Accumula 2

STUDENT BOOK

JUMP Math
One Yonge Street, Suite 1014
Toronto, Ontario M5E 1E5
Canada
www.jumpmath.org

Writers: Dr. Heather Betel, Dr. Francisco Kibedi, Julie Lorinc, Dr. John Mighton
Consultants: Dr. Anna Klebanov, Dr. Sindi Sabourin
Editors: Megan Burns, Liane Tsui, Natalie Francis, Annie Chern, Julia Cochrane, Janice Dyer, Dawn Hunter, Neomi Majmudar, Una Malcolm, Rita Vanden Heuvel
Layout and Illustrations: Linh Lam, Sawyer Paul, Gabriella Kerr, Pam Lostracco
Cover Design: Sunday Lek
Cover Photograph: © Freepik.com

ISBN 978-1-77395-294-9

First printing January 2024

Parts of this material were first published in 2014 in AP Book 2.1, US edition (978-1-927457-37-5) and AP Book 2.2, US edition (978-1-927457-38-2).

Printed and bound in Canada

Welcome to JUMP Math!

Entering the world of JUMP Math means believing that every learner has the capacity to be fully numerate and love math.

The **JUMP Math Accumula Student Book** is the companion to the **JUMP Math Accumula** supplementary resource for Grades 1 to 8, which is designed to strengthen foundational math knowledge and prepare all students for success in understanding math problems at grade level. This book provides opportunities for students to consolidate learning by exploring important math concepts through independent practice.

Unique Evidence-Based Approach and Resources

JUMP Math's unique approach, Kindergarten to Grade 8 resources, and professional learning for teachers have been producing positive learning outcomes for children and teachers in classrooms in Canada, the United States, and other countries for over 20 years. Our resources are aligned with the science on how children's brains learn best and have been demonstrated through studies to greatly improve problem solving, computation, and fluency skills. (See our research at **jumpmath.org**.) Our approach is designed to build equity by supporting the full spectrum of learners to achieve success in math.

Confidence Building is Key

JUMP Math begins each grade with review to enable every student to quickly develop the confidence needed to engage deeply with math. Our distinctive incremental approach to learning math concepts gradually increases the level of difficulty for students, empowering them to become motivated, independent problem solvers. Our books are also designed with simple pictures and models to avoid overwhelming learners when introducing new concepts, enabling them to see the deep structure of the math and gain the confidence to solve a wide range of math problems.

About JUMP Math

JUMP Math is a non-profit organization dedicated to helping every child in every classroom develop confidence, understanding, and a love of math. JUMP Math also offers a comprehensive set of classroom resources for students in Kindergarten to Grade 8.

For more information, visit JUMP Math at: www.jumpmath.org.

Contents

I. The Next Number

Write the next number.

1. 4, _5_

2. 2, _____

3. 8, _____

4. 5, _____

5. 3, _____

6. 7, _____

7. 6, _____

8. 1, _____

Write the next number.

9. 3, _4_

23, _24_

10. 7, _____

47, _____

11. 5, _____

35, _____

12. 2, _____

72, _____

13. 8, _____

18, _____

14. 6, _____

86, _____

15. 4, _____

54, _____

16. 1, _____

91, _____

Write the next two numbers.

17. 2, _3_, _4_

52, _53_, _54_

18. 1, _____, _____

21, _____, _____

19. 7, _____, _____

47, _____, _____

20. 3, _____, _____

93, _____, _____

21. 6, _____, _____

76, _____, _____

22. 5, _____, _____

85, _____, _____

◯ Write the next three numbers.

23.

3, _4_ , _5_ , _6_   23, _24_ , _25_ , _26_   63, _64_ , _65_ , _66_

24.

16, ____, ____, ____   36, ____, ____, ____   76, ____, ____, ____

25.

24, ____, ____, ____   54, ____, ____, ____   84, ____, ____, ____

26.

1, ____, ____, ____   41, ____, ____, ____   91, ____, ____, ____

27.

15, ____, ____, ____   65, ____, ____, ____   75, ____, ____, ____

◯ Write the next four numbers.

28.

25, ____, ____, ____, ____   45, ____, ____, ____, ____

29.

13, ____, ____, ____, ____   73, ____, ____, ____, ____

30.

41, ____, ____, ____, ____   91, ____, ____, ____, ____

31.

2, ____, ____, ____, ____   82, ____, ____, ____, ____

2   JUMP Math Accumula

2. Addition

☐ Add.

1.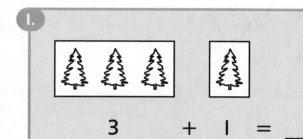

$$3 \quad + \quad 1 \quad = \quad \underline{\ 4\ }$$

2.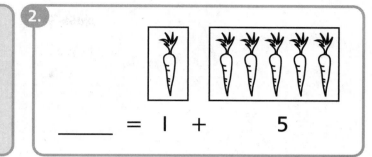

$$\underline{\qquad} = 1 \quad + \quad 5$$

3.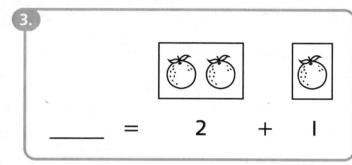

$$\underline{\qquad} = \quad 2 \quad + \quad 1$$

4.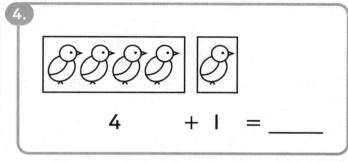

$$4 \quad + 1 \quad = \underline{\qquad}$$

5.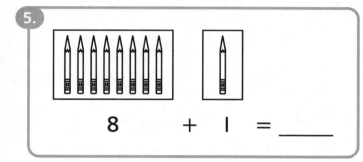

$$8 \quad + \quad 1 \quad = \underline{\qquad}$$

6.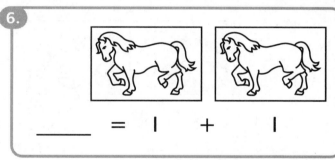

$$\underline{\qquad} = 1 \quad + \quad 1$$

7.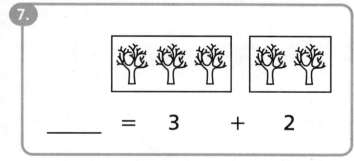

$$\underline{\qquad} = \quad 3 \quad + \quad 2$$

8.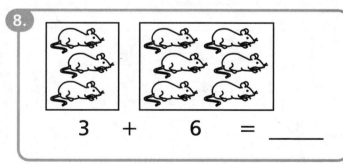

$$3 \quad + \quad 6 \quad = \underline{\qquad}$$

9.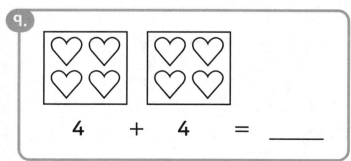

$$4 \quad + \quad 4 \quad = \underline{\qquad}$$

10.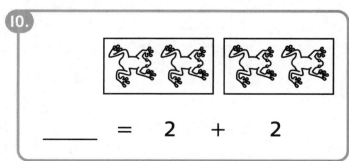

$$\underline{\qquad} = \quad 2 \quad + \quad 2$$

☐ **Add.**

11.

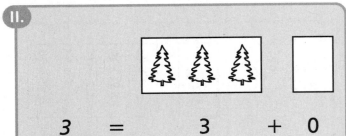

_3_ = 3 + 0

12.

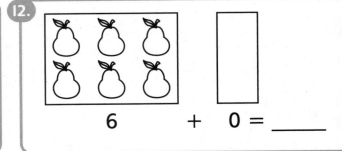

6 + 0 = ____

13.

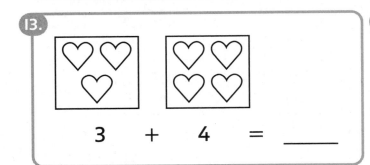

3 + 4 = ____

14.

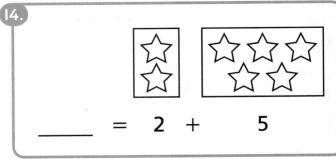

____ = 2 + 5

15.

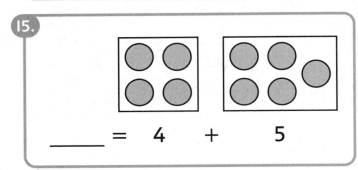

____ = 4 + 5

16.

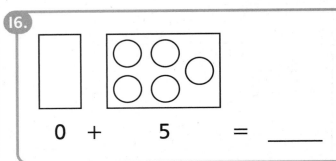

0 + 5 = ____

17.

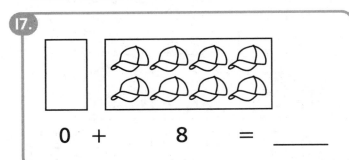

0 + 8 = ____

18.

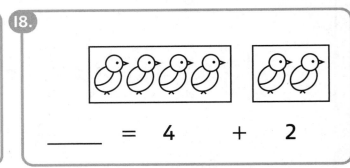

____ = 4 + 2

19.

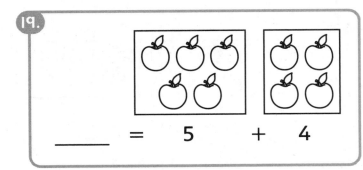

____ = 5 + 4

20.

7 + 2 = ____

3. Adding by Counting On

☐ Add 1 by counting on.

1.

3 + 1 = _____

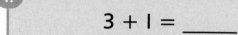

3   4

so 3 + 1 = __4__

13 + 1 = _____

13   14

so 13 + 1 = __14__

2.

7 + 1 = _____   47 + 1 = _____   87 + 1 = _____

3.

_____ = 2 + 1   _____ = 32 + 1   _____ = 62 + 1

☐ Add 2 by counting on.

4.

6 + 2 = _____

6   7   8

so 6 + 2 = __8__

56 + 2 = _____

56   57   58

so 56 + 2 = __58__

5.

3 + 2 = _____   53 + 2 = _____   63 + 2 = _____

6.

_____ = 15 + 2   _____ = 35 + 2   _____ = 75 + 2

○ Add 3 by counting on.

7.

2 + 3 = _____

2   3   4   5

so 2 + 3 = __5__

12 + 3 = _____

12   13   14   15

so 12 + 3 = __15__

8.

4 + 3 = _____   54 + 3 = _____   74 + 3 = _____

9.

_____ = 21 + 3   _____ = 41 + 3   _____ = 81 + 3

10.

5 + 3 = _____   55 + 3 = _____   65 + 3 = _____

11.

_____ = 6 + 3   _____ = 46 + 3   _____ = 96 + 3

12. BONUS

110 + 3 = __113__   140 + 3 = _____   170 + 3 = _____

13. BONUS

_____ = 230 + 3   _____ = 250 + 3   _____ = 280 + 3

4. Even and Odd Numbers

☐ Count the stars.
☐ Pair up as many stars as you can.
☐ Write **even** if you can pair all the stars.
   Write **odd** if you cannot.

1.
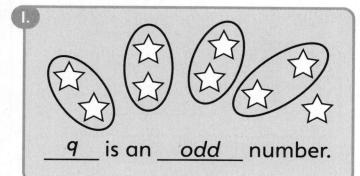
__9__ is an __odd__ number.

2.

_____ is an _____ number.

3.

_____ is an _____ number.

4.
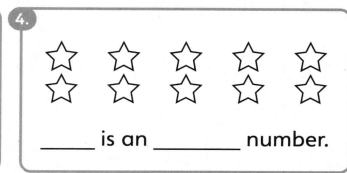
_____ is an _____ number.

5.
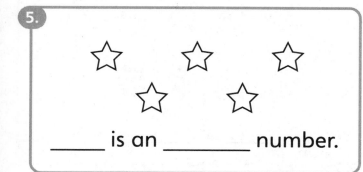
_____ is an _____ number.

6.

_____ is an _____ number.

7.
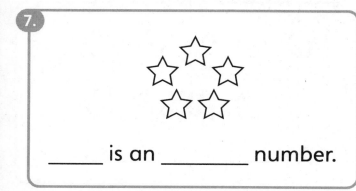
_____ is an _____ number.

8.
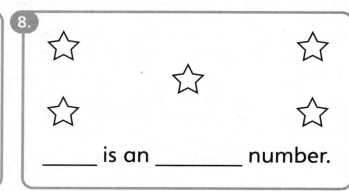
_____ is an _____ number.

☐ Draw a line to divide the dots into 2 equal groups if you can.

☐ Write **even** if you can divide the dots equally.
   Write **odd** if you cannot.

9.

8 is ___even___.

10.

7 is ___odd___.

11.

6 is _____.

12.

3 is _____.

13.

____ is _____.

14.

____ is _____.

15.

____ is _____.

16.

____ is _____.

17.

____ is _____.

5. Patterns with Even and Odd Numbers

◯ Pair the faces up.
◯ Write **even** if you can pair all the objects.
   Write **odd** if you cannot.

1.

1 is _____.

2.

2 is _____.

3.

3 is _____.

4.

4 is _____.

5.

5 is _____.

6.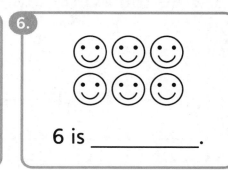

6 is _____.

7.

7 is _____.

8.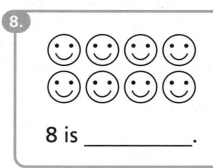

8 is _____.

9.

9 is _____.

◯ Write **O** for odd and **E** for even.
◯ Extend both patterns.

10.

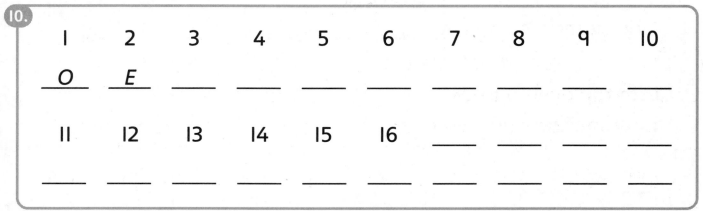

1	2	3	4	5	6	7	8	9	10
_O_	_E_	___	___	___	___	___	___	___	___

11	12	13	14	15	16				
						___	___	___	___

___ ___ ___ ___ ___ ___ ___ ___ ___ ___

◯ Shade the even numbers.
◯ Circle the odd numbers.

11.

1	2	3	4	5	6	7	8	9	10
11	12	13	14	15	16	17	18	19	20
21	22	23	24	25	26	27	28	29	30

◯ Write the even numbers.

12.

_____   _____   _____   _____   _____

_____   _____   _____   _____   _____

_____   _____   _____   _____   _____

◯ Write the odd numbers.

13.

_____   _____   _____   _____   _____

_____   _____   _____   _____   _____

_____   _____   _____   _____   _____

14.

Even numbers end with _____, _____, _____, _____, or _____.

Odd numbers end with _____, _____, _____, _____, or _____.

◯ Circle the even numbers.
◯ Underline the odd numbers.

15.

5   (2)   8   1   6   4   3   7   10   9

6. The Next or Previous Even or Odd Number

☐ Write the next even number.

1. 6, _____

2. 8, _____

3. 4, _____

4. 2, _____

5. 16, _____

6. 24, _____

7. 20, _____

8. 14, _____

☐ Write the next odd number.

9. 7, _____

10. 1, _____

11. 5, _____

12. 3, _____

13. 11, _____

14. 23, _____

15. 27, _____

16. 15, _____

☐ Write the even number before.

17. _____, 6

18. _____, 4

19. _____, 8

20. _____, 10

21. _____, 22

22. _____, 12

23. _____, 26

24. _____, 16

☐ Write the odd number before.

25. _____, 9

26. _____, 3

27. _____, 5

28. _____, 7

29. _____, 13

30. _____, 29

31. _____, 17

32. _____, 25

◯ Write the next even number.

◯ Write an addition sentence to show adding 2.

33.
6, _8_   _6_ + _2_ = _8_

34.
4, ____   ____ + ____ = ____

35.
10, ____   ____ + ____ = ____

36.
12, ____   ____ + ____ = ____

◯ Write the next even number.

37.
2, _4_

12, _14_

22, _24_

32, _34_

42, _44_

52, _54_

62, _64_

72, _74_

82, _84_

92, _94_

38.
6, ____

16, ____

26, ____

36, ____

46, ____

56, ____

66, ____

76, ____

86, ____

96, ____

39.
4, ____

14, ____

24, ____

34, ____

44, ____

54, ____

64, ____

74, ____

84, ____

94, ____

40.
8, _10_

18, _20_

28, ____

38, ____

48, ____

58, ____

68, ____

78, ____

88, ____

98, ____

Write the next odd number.

Write an addition sentence to show adding 2.

41.
5, _7_   _5_ + _2_ = _7_

42.
3, ____   ____ + ____ = ____

43.
11, ____   ____ + ____ = ____

44.
17, ____   ____ + ____ = ____

Write the next odd number.

45.
3, _5_

13, _15_

23, _25_

33, _35_

46.
7, ____

17, ____

27, ____

37, ____

47.
9, _11_

19, ____

29, ____

39, ____

48.
5, ____

15, ____

25, ____

35, ____

Do you add 1 or 2 to get the answer?

49.
$5 + \underline{1} = 6$

50.
$2 + \underline{2} = 4$

51.
$7 + \underline{} = 9$

52.
$16 + \underline{} = 18$

53.
$15 + \underline{} = 16$

54.
$8 + \underline{} = 9$

55.
$10 + \underline{} = 11$

56.
$11 + \underline{} = 13$

57.
$18 + \underline{} = 20$

7. Order in Adding

How many dots are on each side of the domino?
☐ Add the dots to find the total.

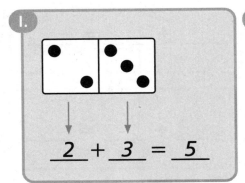

2 + 3 = 5

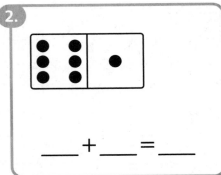

___ + ___ = ___

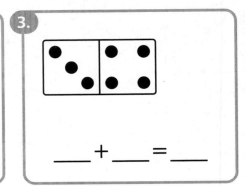

___ + ___ = ___

Ben turned the domino around.
Did the number of dots change?
☐ Circle **Yes** or **No**.

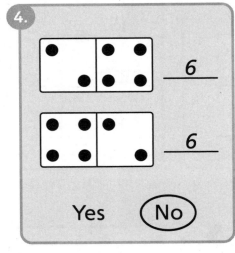

Yes   (No)

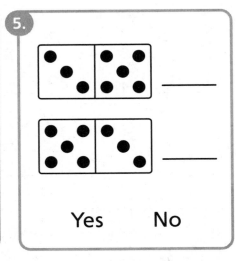

Yes   No

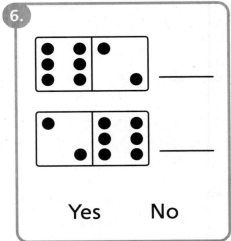

Yes   No

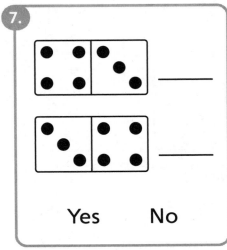

Yes   No

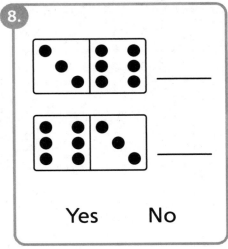

Yes   No

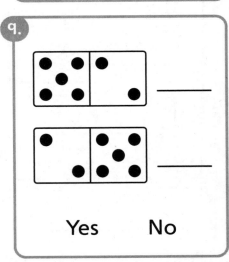

Yes   No

Rosa turned the domino around.
☐ Write two addition sentences.

10.

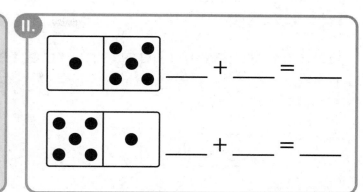

_2_ + _1_ = _3_

_1_ + _2_ = _3_

11.

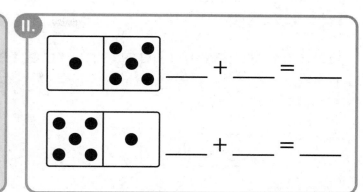

___ + ___ = ___

___ + ___ = ___

12.

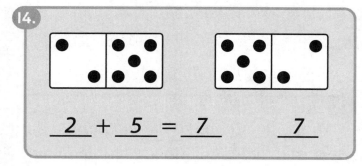

___ + ___ = ___

___ + ___ = ___

13.

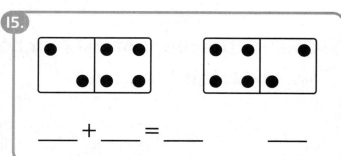

___ + ___ = ___

___ + ___ = ___

Ali turned the domino around.
☐ Add the dots on the first domino.
☐ How many dots are on the other domino?

14.

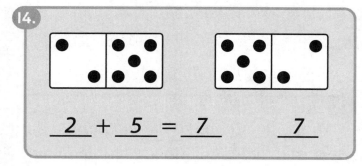

_2_ + _5_ = _7_   _7_

15.

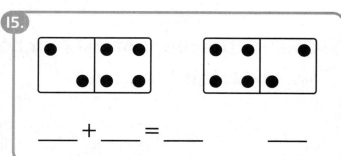

___ + ___ = ___   ___

16.

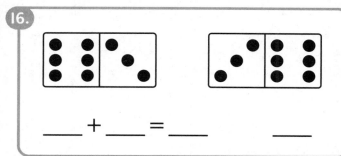

___ + ___ = ___   ___

17.

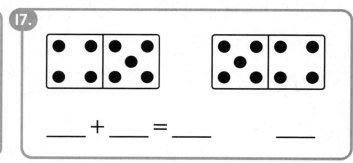

___ + ___ = ___   ___

- ☐ Add.
- ☐ Change the order of the numbers.
- ☐ Add again.
- ☐ Did the answer change? Circle **Yes** or **No**.

18.

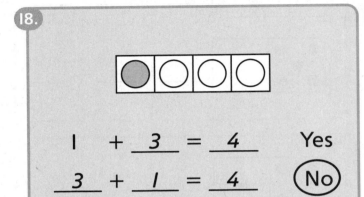

$1 + \underline{3} = \underline{4}$ Yes

$\underline{3} + \underline{1} = \underline{4}$ (No)

19.

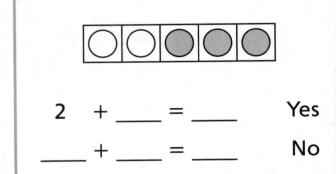

$2 + \underline{\hphantom{00}} = \underline{\hphantom{00}}$ Yes

$\underline{\hphantom{00}} + \underline{\hphantom{00}} = \underline{\hphantom{00}}$ No

20.

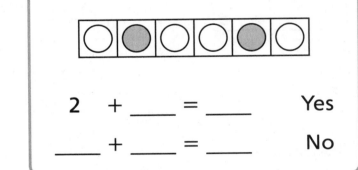

$2 + \underline{\hphantom{00}} = \underline{\hphantom{00}}$ Yes

$\underline{\hphantom{00}} + \underline{\hphantom{00}} = \underline{\hphantom{00}}$ No

21.

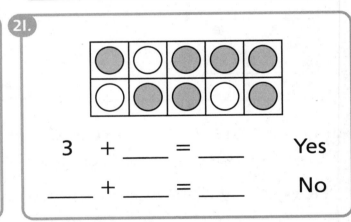

$3 + \underline{\hphantom{00}} = \underline{\hphantom{00}}$ Yes

$\underline{\hphantom{00}} + \underline{\hphantom{00}} = \underline{\hphantom{00}}$ No

- ☐ Change the order of the numbers.
- ☐ Are the totals the same?

22.

$5 + 1 = \underline{6}$ (Yes)

$\underline{1} + \underline{5} = \underline{6}$ No

23.

$5 + 2 = \underline{\hphantom{00}}$ Yes

$\underline{\hphantom{00}} + \underline{\hphantom{00}} = \underline{\hphantom{00}}$ No

24.

$7 + 1 = \underline{\hphantom{00}}$ Yes

$\underline{\hphantom{00}} + \underline{\hphantom{00}} = \underline{\hphantom{00}}$ No

25.

$4 + 2 = \underline{\hphantom{00}}$ Yes

$\underline{\hphantom{00}} + \underline{\hphantom{00}} = \underline{\hphantom{00}}$ No

JUMP Math Accumula

8. First Word Problems

Add using the pictures.

1.
4 bunnies   2 more bunnies

$$4 + 2 = \rule{2cm}{0.4pt}$$

2.
3 bunnies   1 more bunny

$$3 + 1 = \rule{2cm}{0.4pt}$$

3.
1 bunny   5 more bunnies

$$1 + 5 = \rule{2cm}{0.4pt}$$

4.
2 bunnies   6 more bunnies

 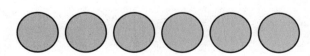

$$2 + 6 = \rule{2cm}{0.4pt}$$

☐ Add using the pictures.

5.

3 big frogs　　　　and　　　　2 small frogs

3 + 2 = _____ frogs altogether

6.

I big frog　　　　and　　　　4 small frogs

I + 4 = _____ frogs altogether

7.

5 big frogs　　　　and　　　　3 small frogs

5 + 3 = _____ frogs altogether

8.

2 small frogs　　　　and　　　　7 big frogs

2 + 7 = _____ frogs altogether

☐ Draw circles to show the numbers.
☐ Add.

9.
There are 4 cats.   Then 2 more cats come.

___ ___ ___ ___   ___ ___

4 + 2 = _____ cats altogether

10.
4 large dogs   and   3 small dogs

___ ___ ___ ___ ___ ___ ___

4 + 3 = _____ dogs altogether

11.
There are 3 glasses of milk. Nina brings 2 more glasses of milk.

___ ___ ___   ___ ___

3 + 2 = _____ glasses altogether

12.
6 small birds   and   2 large birds

___ ___ ___ ___ ___ ___ ___

6 + 2 = _____ birds altogether

9. Equal (=) and Not Equal (≠)

Do the tables have the same number of balls?

☐ If they do, circle =.

☐ If they do not, circle ≠.

1.
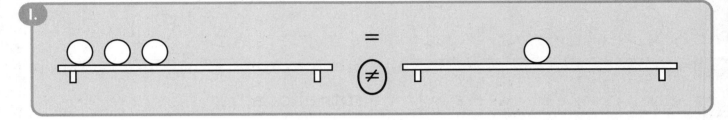

2.
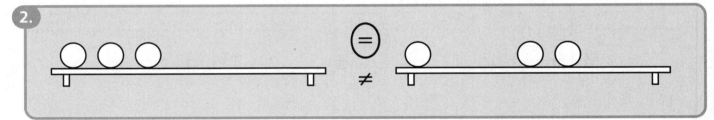

3.
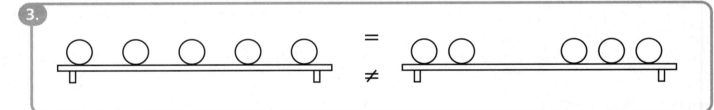

4.
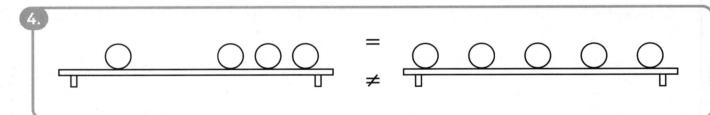

5.
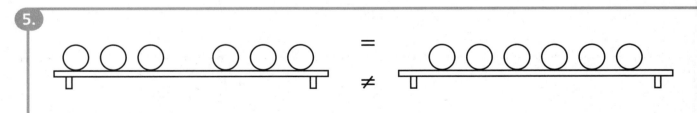

6.
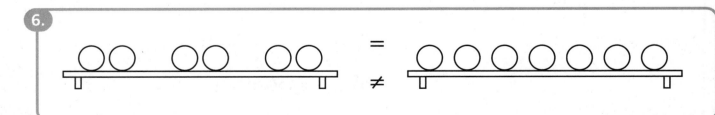

☐ Write the number of balls.

☐ Write = or ≠ in the box.

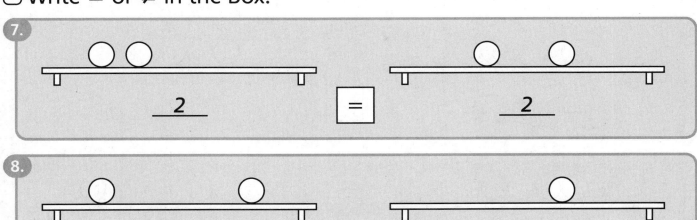

7.

_2_   =   _2_

8.

_2_   ≠   _1_

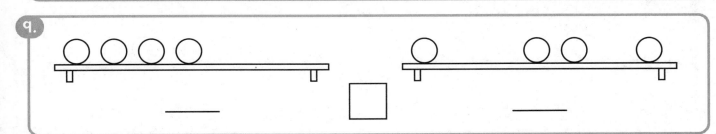

9.

_____   ☐   _____

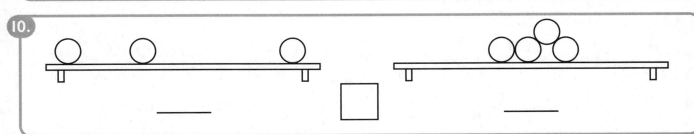

10.

_____   ☐   _____

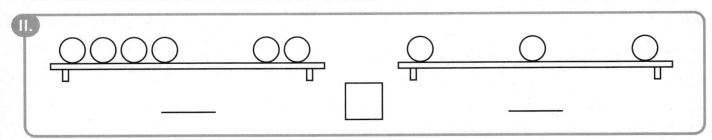

11.

_____   ☐   _____

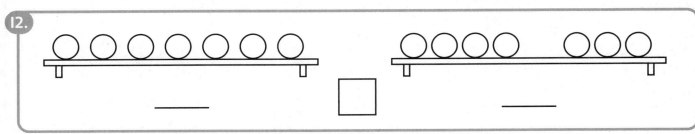

12.

_____   ☐   _____

☐ Write the number of balls.

☐ Write = or ≠ in the box.

13.
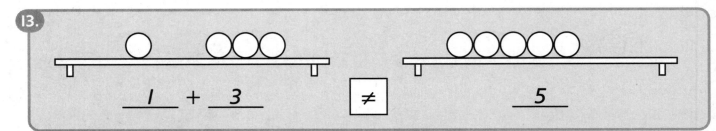

___1___ + ___3___   ≠   ___5___

14.
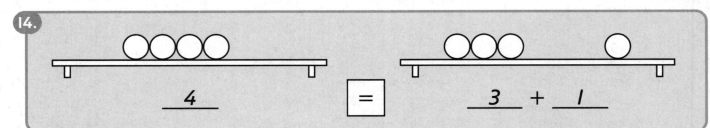

___4___   =   ___3___ + ___1___

15.
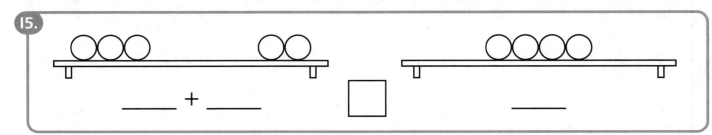

_____ + _____   ☐   _____

16.
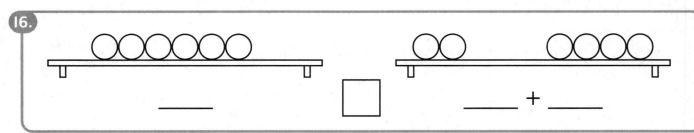

_____   ☐   _____ + _____

17.
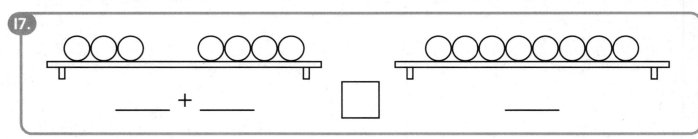

_____ + _____   ☐   _____

18.
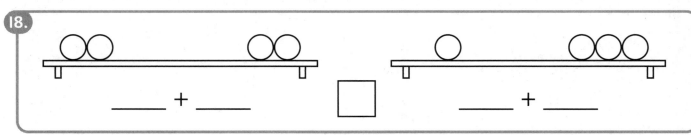

_____ + _____   ☐   _____ + _____

☐ Circle the correct addition sentence.

19.
6   =   2 + 1

(6   ≠   2 + 1)

20.
(4   =   2 + 2)

4   ≠   2 + 2

21.
2 + 1   =   3

2 + 1   ≠   3

22.
2 + 2   =   5

2 + 2   ≠   5

23.
6   =   5 + 1

6   ≠   5 + 1

24.
6   =   4 + 3

6   ≠   4 + 3

25.
8 + 2   =   9

8 + 2   ≠   9

26.
3 + 5   =   8

3 + 5   ≠   8

27.
10   =   4 + 6

10   ≠   4 + 6

28.
7   =   2 + 7

7   ≠   2 + 7

29.
4 + 5   =   9

4 + 5   ≠   9

30.
4 + 7   =   10

4 + 7   ≠   10

10. Using Doubles to Add (I)

◯ Write a doubles sentence.

1.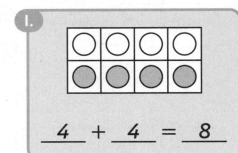

___4___ + ___4___ = ___8___

2.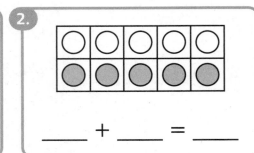

_____ + _____ = _____

3.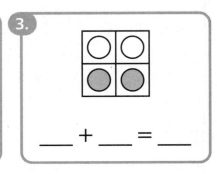

_____ + ___ = _____

4.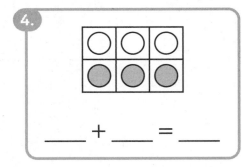

_____ + _____ = _____

5.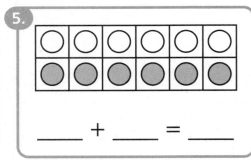

_____ + _____ = _____

6.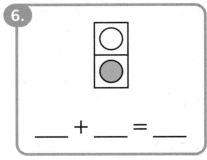

_____ + ___ = _____

◯ Write a doubles addition sentence.

7. Jake has 3 cats. Grace has 3 cats.

Altogether, they have ___3___ + ___3___ = ___6___ cats.

8. Tina has 2 books. Sun has 2 books.

Altogether, they have _____ + _____ = _____ books.

9. Ivan has 5 pencils. Emma has 5 pencils.

Altogether, they have _____ + _____ = _____ pencils.

10. Alex has 4 hats. Raj has 4 hats.

Altogether, they have _____ + _____ = _____ hats.

⬭ Write an addition for each picture.

Are the two additions equal?

⬭ If they are, circle =. If they are not, circle ≠.

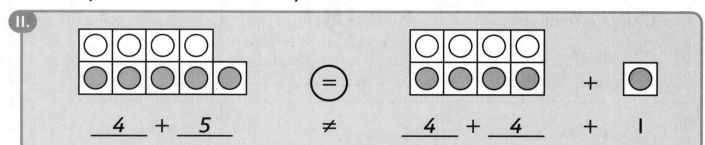

11.

___4___ + ___5___   ≠   ___4___ + ___4___   +   1
    ⊜ (=)

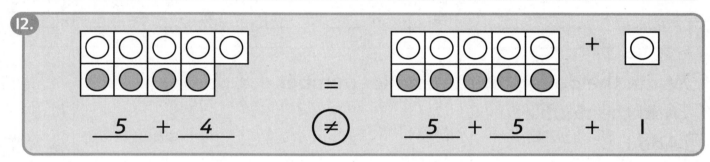

12.

___5___ + ___4___   =   ___5___ + ___5___   +   1
    ⊜ (≠)

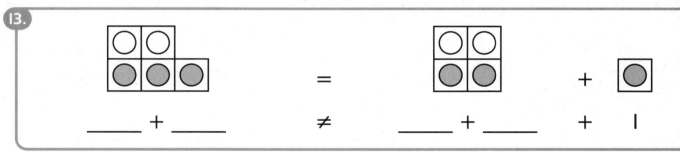

13.

_____ + _____   =   _____ + _____   +   1
    ≠

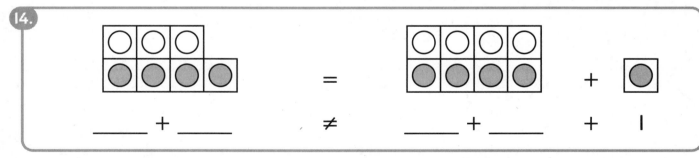

14.

_____ + _____   =   _____ + _____   +   1
    ≠

15.

_____ + _____   =   _____ + _____   +   1
    ≠

○ Circle the smaller number.
○ Write the double of the smaller number plus I.

16.
$(5) + 6$
$= \underline{5} + \underline{5} + \underline{1}$

17.
$6 + (5)$
$= \underline{5} + \underline{5} + \underline{1}$

18.
$4 + 3$
$= \underline{} + \underline{} + \underline{}$

19.
$3 + 4$
$= \underline{} + \underline{} + \underline{}$

20.
$6 + 7$
$= \underline{} + \underline{} + \underline{}$

21.
$7 + 6$
$= \underline{} + \underline{} + \underline{}$

○ Write the double of the smaller number.
○ Add the double.
○ Add I.

22.
$4 + 5$
$= \underline{4} + \underline{4} + 1$
$= \underline{8} + 1$
$= \underline{9}$

23.
$5 + 4$
$= \underline{} + \underline{} + 1$
$= \underline{} + 1$
$= \underline{}$

24.
$2 + 3$
$= \underline{} + \underline{} + 1$
$= \underline{} + 1$
$= \underline{}$

25.
$3 + 2$
$= \underline{} + \underline{} + 1$
$= \underline{} + 1$
$= \underline{}$

26.
$5 + 6$
$= \underline{} + \underline{} + 1$
$= \underline{} + 1$
$= \underline{}$

27.
$6 + 5$
$= \underline{} + \underline{} + 1$
$= \underline{} + 1$
$= \underline{}$

II. Using Doubles to Add (2)

☐ Write the number that is between.

1. 5, __6__ , 7

2. 1, _____ , 3

3. 6, _____ , 8

4. 7 and 9   __8__

5. 4 and 6   _____

6. 8 and 10   _____

☐ Write an addition for each picture.

7.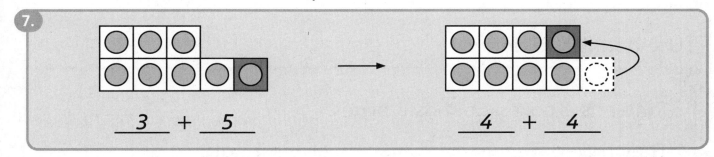

__3__ + __5__   __4__ + __4__

8.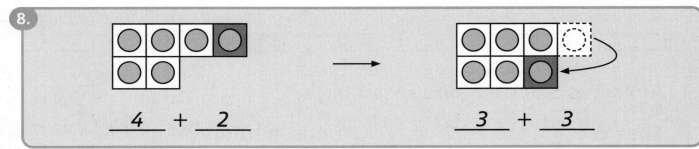

__4__ + __2__   __3__ + __3__

9.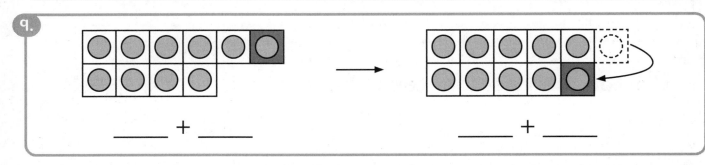

_____ + _____   _____ + _____

10.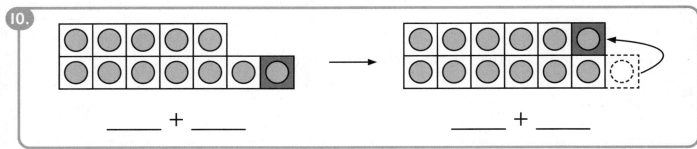

_____ + _____   _____ + _____

◯ Write the addition as a double.

11.

$3 + 5$ $=$ ___4___ $+$ ___4___

$=$ ___8___

12.

$1 + 3$ $=$ _____ $+$ _____

$=$ _____

13.

$6 + 8$ $=$ _____ $+$ _____

$=$ _____

14.

$5 + 7$ $=$ _____ $+$ _____

$=$ _____

◯ Use doubles to add.

15.

Jane has 4 boxes. Sal has 6 boxes.

They have _____ $+$ _____ $=$ _____ boxes in total.

16.

Amit sees 5 birds. Mona sees 3 birds.

They see _____ $+$ _____ $=$ _____ birds in total.

17.

Kim counts 5 cars. Tony counts 7 cars.

They count _____ $+$ _____ $=$ _____ cars in total.

18.

Vicky plants 1 tree. John plants 3 trees.

They plant _____ $+$ _____ $=$ _____ trees in total.

12. Distance from 0 on a Number Line

☐ Circle the correct number line.

1.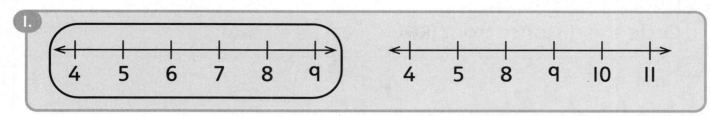

2.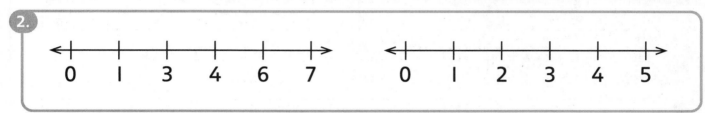

3.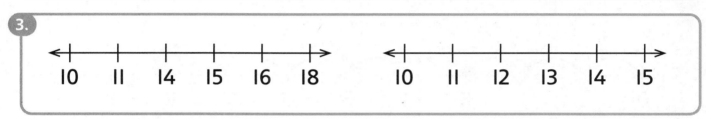

The frog starts at 0.

☐ Number each jump.

☐ Circle the distance from 0.

4.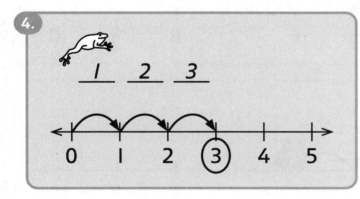

5.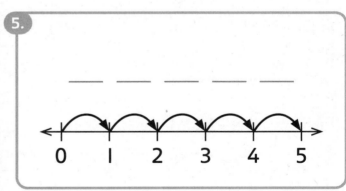

6.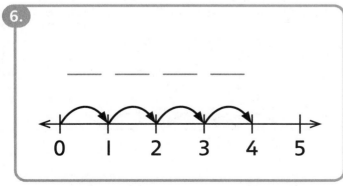

7.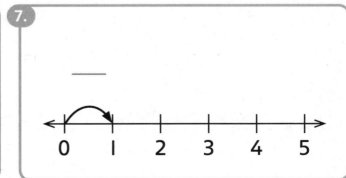

How many jumps away from 0 is the frog?

☐ Number each jump.

☐ Circle the distance from 0.

8.

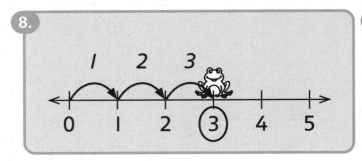

9.

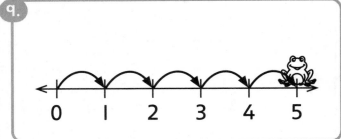

10.

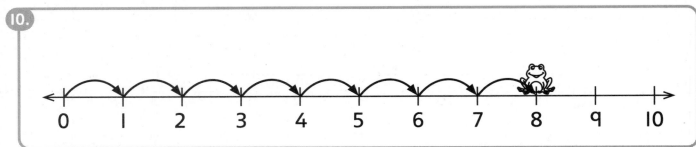

11.

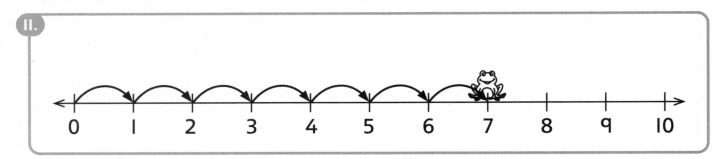

12.

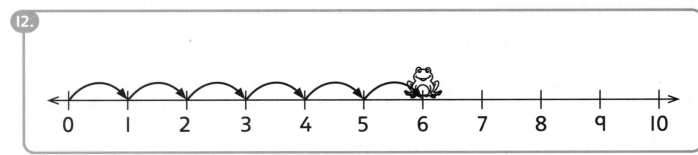

13.

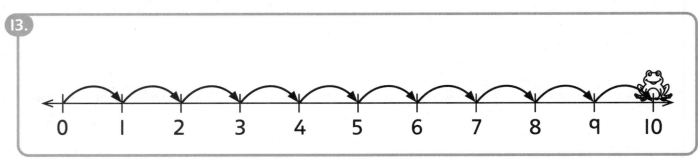

13. Number Words from 0 to 10

☐ Match the numbers to the words.

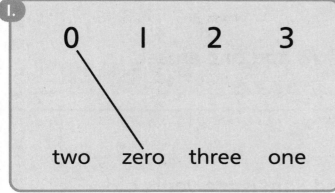

1.

0   1   2   3

two   zero   three   one

2.

5   6   8   9

nine   eight   six   five

3.

4   7   6   8   3   9

seven   three   four   nine   six   eight

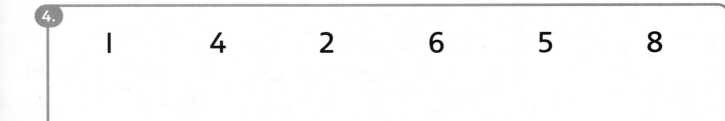

4.

1   4   2   6   5   8

six   one   two   eight   four   five

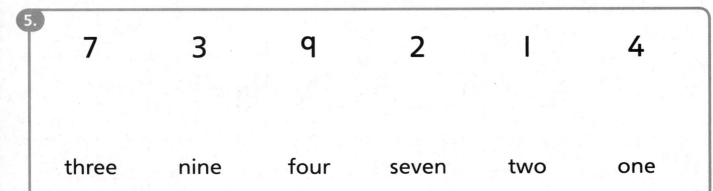

5.

7   3   9   2   1   4

three   nine   four   seven   two   one

○ Write the numbers above the number words.

6.

$$8 \qquad\qquad I$$

Hanna has eight pencils and one eraser.

7.

Amit is nine years old and Sam is ten years old.

8.

Pam has seven crayons, two markers, and zero pens.

9.

Rob has five brothers and his sister has six brothers.

10.

Liz has three sisters and her brother has four sisters.

○ Circle the number words.

11.

(three) (two) (nine) (six) (eight)

12.

t e n s e v e n f i v e f o u r o n e t h r e e

14. Number Words from 0 to 20

⬜ Underline the beginning letters that are the same.

1. <u>tw</u>o   <u>tw</u>elve

2. six   sixteen

3. three   thirteen

4. four   fourteen

5. eight   eighteen

6. five   fifteen

⬜ Circle the digits that are the same.

7. ②   1②

8. 6   16

9. 7   17

10. 9   19

11. 8   18

12. 3   13

⬜ Underline and circle the same parts.

13. <u>three</u> = ③
    <u>thi</u>rteen = 1③

14. four = 4
    fourteen = 14

15. five = 5
    fifteen = 15

16. nine = 9
    nineteen = 19

17. seven = 7
    seventeen = 17

18. two = 2
    twelve = 12

Write the number.

19. thirteen = _1_ _3_

20. seventeen = ___ ___

21. fifteen = ___ ___

22. sixteen = ___ ___

23. fourteen = ___ ___

24. twelve = ___ ___

25. nineteen = ___ ___

26. eighteen = ___ ___

27. eleven = ___ ___

Match the word with the number.

28.

3	6	9	12	15

nine   fifteen   three   six   twelve

29.

11	13	15	17	19

fifteen   nineteen   thirteen   eleven   seventeen

⬡ Write the number above the number word.

30.

13
Clara is thirteen months old.

31.

Mike has twenty teeth.

32.

Sixteen friends played tag.

33.

Holidays start in eleven days.

34.

We played basketball for fifteen minutes.

35.

Will invited eighteen friends to his birthday party.

36. BONUS

Bianca's soccer team has twelve players.

There are seven girls and five boys.

37. BONUS

There are eight pears and twelve plums on the table.

38. BONUS

One week has seven days. Two days are on the weekend.

⬜ Answer the question using the number and the word.

39.
What grade are you in? __2__ = ____two____

40.
How many letters are in your first name? _____ = _____

41.
How old are you? _____ = _____

42.
How many pets do you have? _____ = _____

43.
How many girls are in your class? _____ = _____

44.
How many boys are in your class? _____ = _____

45.
How many months are in a year? _____ = _____

46.
How many blank lines (__) are on this page? _____ = _____

47. BONUS
How many letters are black? _____ = _____

a **b c d** e **f g h** i **j k l m n** o **p q r s t** u **v w x** y **z**

COPYRIGHT © JUMP MATH: NOT TO BE COPIED. US EDITION

JUMP Math Accumula

15. Numbers from 10 to 19

Josh has 10 apples.

Josh gets more apples.

 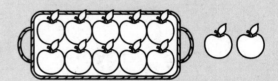

10 + __1__ = __1____1__ apples   10 + __2__ = __1____2__ apples

☐ How many apples altogether? Add.

2.

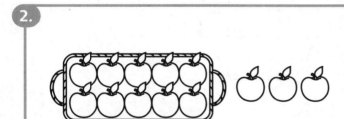

10 + ___ = __1__ ___ apples

3.

10 + ___ = ___ ___ apples

☐ Add.

4.

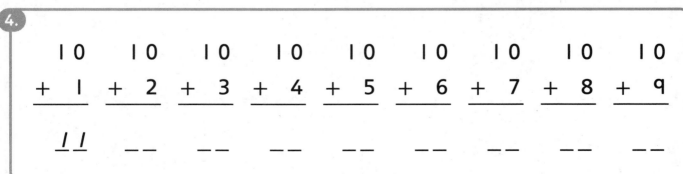

10	10	10	10	10	10	10	10	10
+ 1	+ 2	+ 3	+ 4	+ 5	+ 6	+ 7	+ 8	+ 9
1 1								

⬜ How many?

5.

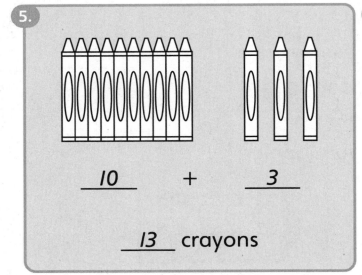

$\underline{\quad 10 \quad}$ + $\underline{\quad 3 \quad}$

$\underline{\quad 13 \quad}$ crayons

6.

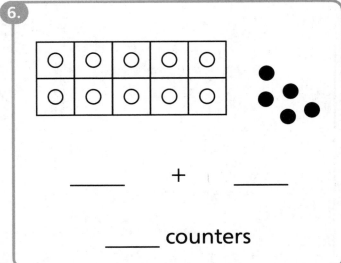

$\underline{\hspace{1.5cm}}$ + $\underline{\hspace{1.5cm}}$

$\underline{\hspace{1.5cm}}$ counters

7.

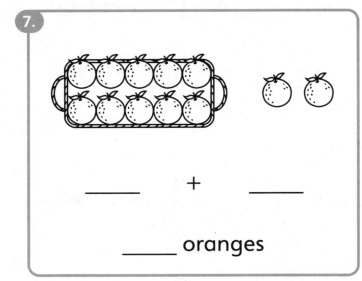

$\underline{\hspace{1.5cm}}$ + $\underline{\hspace{1.5cm}}$

$\underline{\hspace{1.5cm}}$ oranges

8.

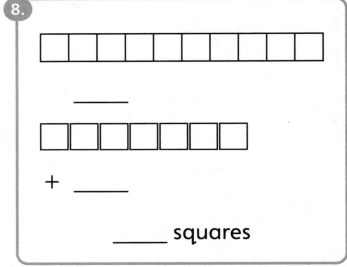

$\underline{\hspace{1.5cm}}$

+ $\underline{\hspace{1.5cm}}$

$\underline{\hspace{1.5cm}}$ squares

9.

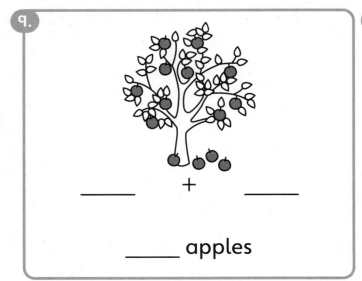

$\underline{\hspace{1.5cm}}$ + $\underline{\hspace{1.5cm}}$

$\underline{\hspace{1.5cm}}$ apples

10.

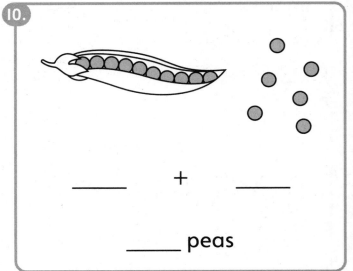

$\underline{\hspace{1.5cm}}$ + $\underline{\hspace{1.5cm}}$

$\underline{\hspace{1.5cm}}$ peas

16. Using 10 to Add

☐ Use the group of 10 to help you add.

1.

7   6

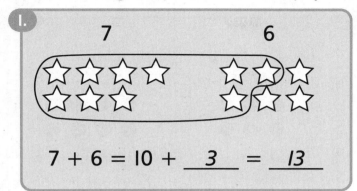

$7 + 6 = 10 +$ __3__ $=$ __13__

2.

8   8

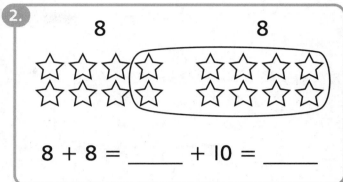

$8 + 8 =$ _____ $+ 10 =$ _____

3.

4   8

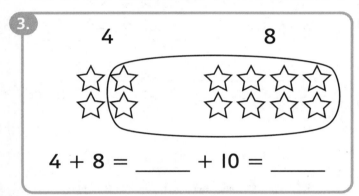

$4 + 8 =$ _____ $+ 10 =$ _____

4.

7   5

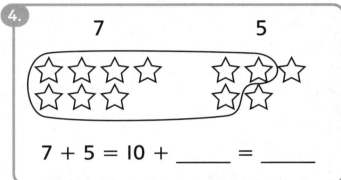

$7 + 5 = 10 +$ _____ $=$ _____

5.

8   6

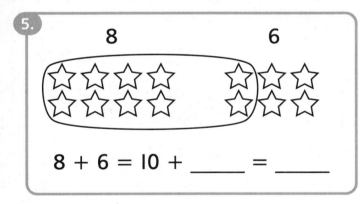

$8 + 6 = 10 +$ _____ $=$ _____

6.

9   7

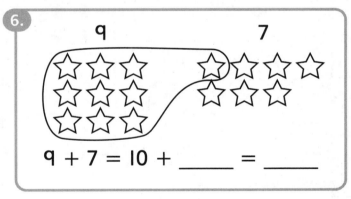

$9 + 7 = 10 +$ _____ $=$ _____

☐ Sara groups 10 in two ways. Does she get the same answer?

7.

3   9

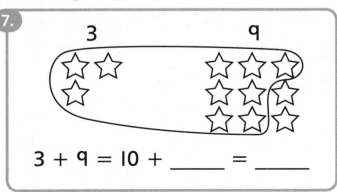

$3 + 9 = 10 +$ _____ $=$ _____

8.

3   9

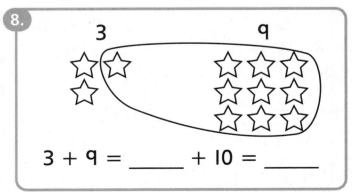

$3 + 9 =$ _____ $+ 10 =$ _____

☐ Circle a group of 10.
☐ Use 10 to add.

9.
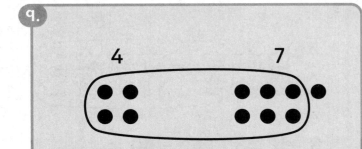

4 + 7 = 10 + ___1___ = ___11___

10.
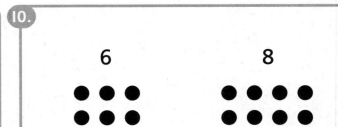

6 + 8 = _____ + 10 = _____

11.
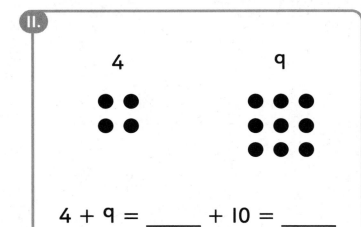

4 + 9 = _____ + 10 = _____

12.

9 + 2 = 10 + _____ = _____

13.
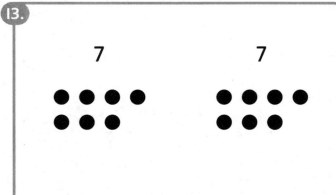

7 + 7 = 10 + _____ = _____

14.
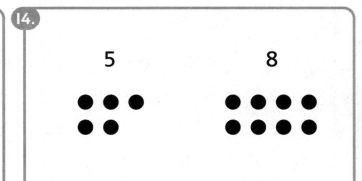

5 + 8 = 10 + _____ = _____

17. Pairs of Numbers That Add to 10

☐ Count on to 10.

1.

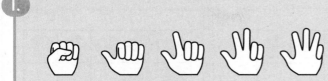

6   _7_   _8_   _9_   _10_   6 + _4_ = 10

5   _6_   _7_   _8_   _9_   _10_   5 + _5_ = 10

2.   5 + _____ = 10

3.   8 + _____ = 10

4.   0 + _____ = 10

5.   4 + _____ = 10

6.   7 + _____ = 10

7.   9 + _____ = 10

☐ Write an addition sentence for the picture.

8.

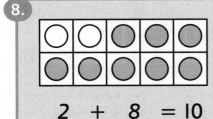

_2_ + _8_ = 10

9.

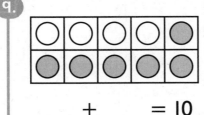

___ + ___ = 10

10.

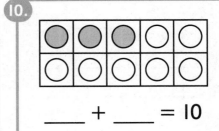

___ + ___ = 10

11.

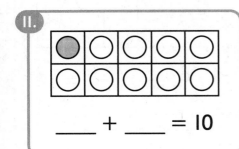

___ + ___ = 10

12.

___ + ___ = 10

13.

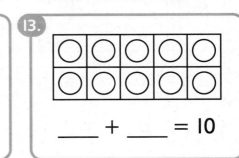

___ + ___ = 10

Draw circles in the empty boxes.

Complete the addition sentence.

14.

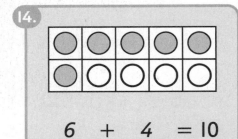

___6___ + ___4___ = 10

15.

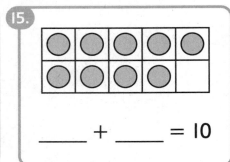

_____ + _____ = 10

16.

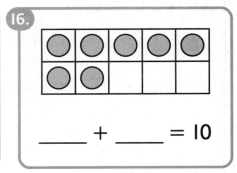

_____ + _____ = 10

17.

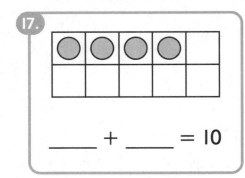

_____ + _____ = 10

18.

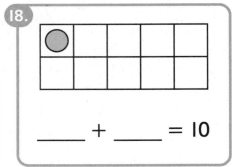

_____ + _____ = 10

19.

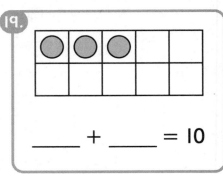

_____ + _____ = 10

Write two addition sentences for the picture.

20.

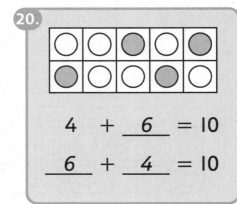

4 + ___6___ = 10

___6___ + ___4___ = 10

21.

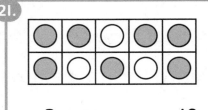

3 + _____ = 10

_____ + _____ = 10

22.

3 + _____ = 10

1 + _____ = 10

_____ + _____ = 10

23.

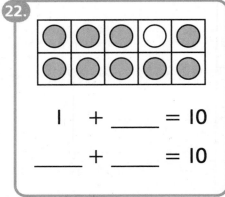

2 + _____ = 10

_____ + _____ = 10

24.

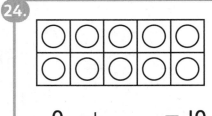

0 + _____ = 10

_____ + _____ = 10

25.

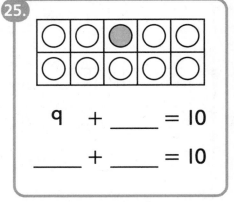

9 + _____ = 10

_____ + _____ = 10

☐ Underline the number that makes 10.
☐ Write the addition sentence.

26.
0 1 ② 3 4 5 6 7 <u>8</u> 9 10   <u>2</u> + <u>8</u> = 10

27.
0 ① 2 3 4 5 6 7 8 9 10   ___ + ___ = 10

28.
0 1 2 3 4 5 ⑥ 7 8 9 10   ___ + ___ = 10

29.
⓪ 1 2 3 4 5 6 7 8 9 10   ___ + ___ = 10

30.
0 1 2 3 4 5 6 ⑦ 8 9 10   ___ + ___ = 10

31.
⑧ 4 9 0 10 5 6 3 <u>2</u> 7 1   <u>8</u> + <u>2</u> = 10

32.
④ 1 5 0 7 9 8 2 10 3 6   ___ + ___ = 10

33.
③ 10 6 1 7 0 8 9 4 5 2   ___ + ___ = 10

34.
⑨ 5 10 1 2 0 3 4 6 8 7   ___ + ___ = 10

35.
⑩ 0 6 5 2 7 1 3 4 8 9   ___ + ___ = 10

18. Using Pictures to Subtract

☐ Use the picture to subtract.

1.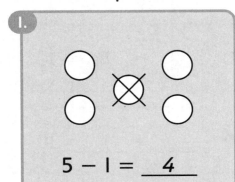

5 – 1 = __4__

2.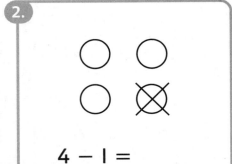

4 – 1 = _____

3.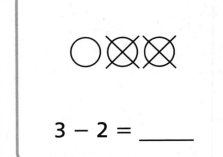

3 – 2 = _____

4.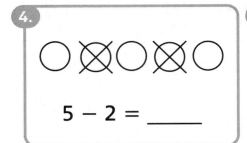

5 – 2 = _____

5.

4 – 3 = _____

6.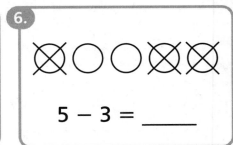

5 – 3 = _____

7.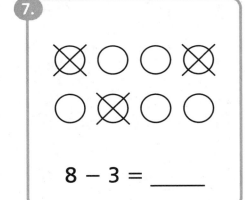

8 – 3 = _____

8.

7 – 4 = _____

9.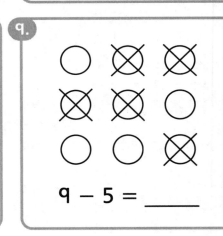

9 – 5 = _____

☐ Write a subtraction sentence for the picture.

10.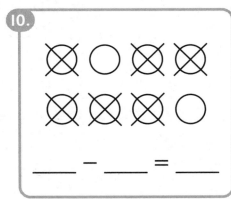

_____ – _____ = _____

11.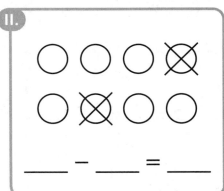

_____ – _____ = _____

12.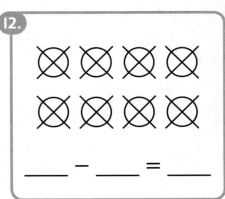

_____ – _____ = _____

☐ Use the picture to subtract.

13.

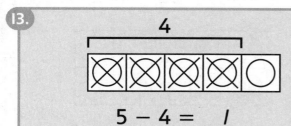

$5 - 4 = \underline{1}$

$5 - 1 = \underline{4}$

14.

$7 - 5 = \underline{}$

$7 - 2 = \underline{}$

15.

$6 - 6 = \underline{}$

$6 - 0 = \underline{}$

☐ Use the picture to subtract the gray circles.

16.

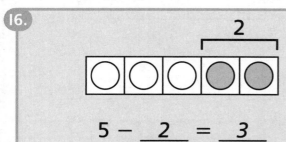

$5 - \underline{2} = \underline{3}$

17.

$5 - \underline{} = \underline{}$

18.

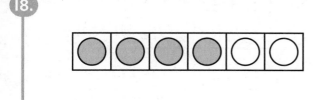

$6 - \underline{} = \underline{}$

19.

$6 - \underline{} = \underline{}$

Write two subtraction sentences.

20.

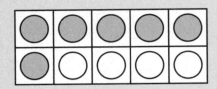

10 − __6__ = __4__

10 − __4__ = __6__

21.

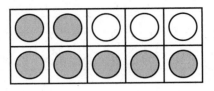

10 − _____ = _____

10 − _____ = _____

22.

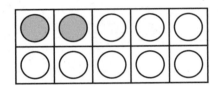

10 − _____ = _____

10 − _____ = _____

23.

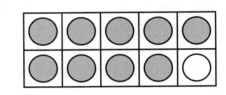

_____ − _____ = _____

_____ − _____ = _____

24.

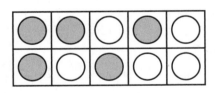

_____ − _____ = _____

_____ − _____ = _____

25.

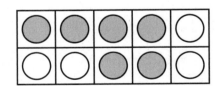

_____ − _____ = _____

_____ − _____ = _____

26.

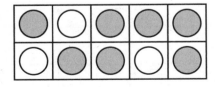

_____ − _____ = _____

_____ − _____ = _____

27.

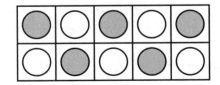

_____ − _____ = _____

_____ − _____ = _____

19. First Word Problems—Subtraction

☐ Subtract.

1.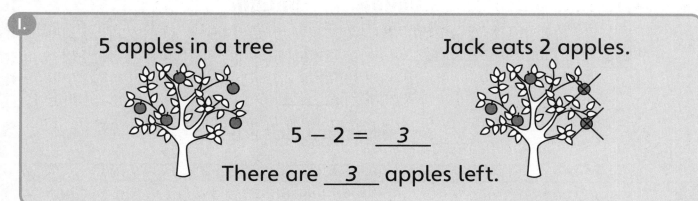

5 apples in a tree

Jack eats 2 apples.

5 − 2 = __3__

There are __3__ apples left.

2.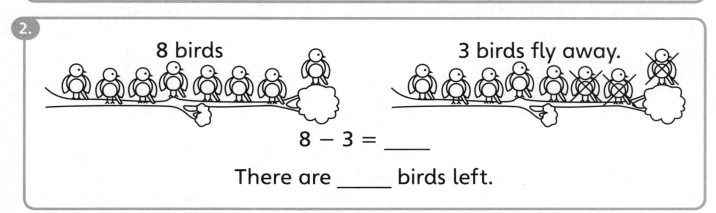

8 birds

3 birds fly away.

8 − 3 = _____

There are _____ birds left.

3.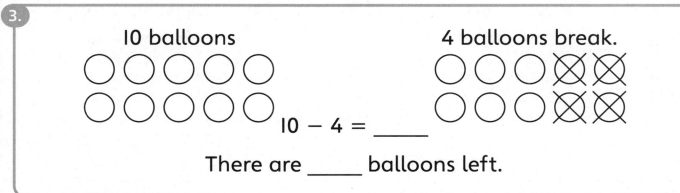

10 balloons

4 balloons break.

10 − 4 = _____

There are _____ balloons left.

4.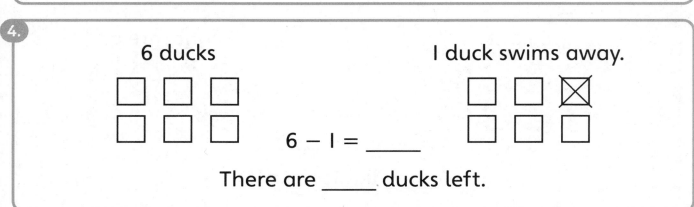

6 ducks

1 duck swims away.

6 − 1 = _____

There are _____ ducks left.

5.

5 windows

2 blinds are open.

5 − 2 = _____

_____ blinds are closed.

6.

4 books

Kate opens 1 book.

4 − 1 = _____

_____ books are closed.

7.

7 new crayons

David uses 2 crayons.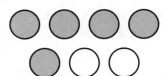

7 − 2 = _____

_____ crayons are not used.

8.

8 lights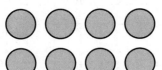

5 lights are on.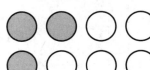

8 − 5 = _____

_____ lights are off.

20. Blocks in a Bag

Some blocks are in the bag.

☐ Circle the table where you know the exact number of blocks.

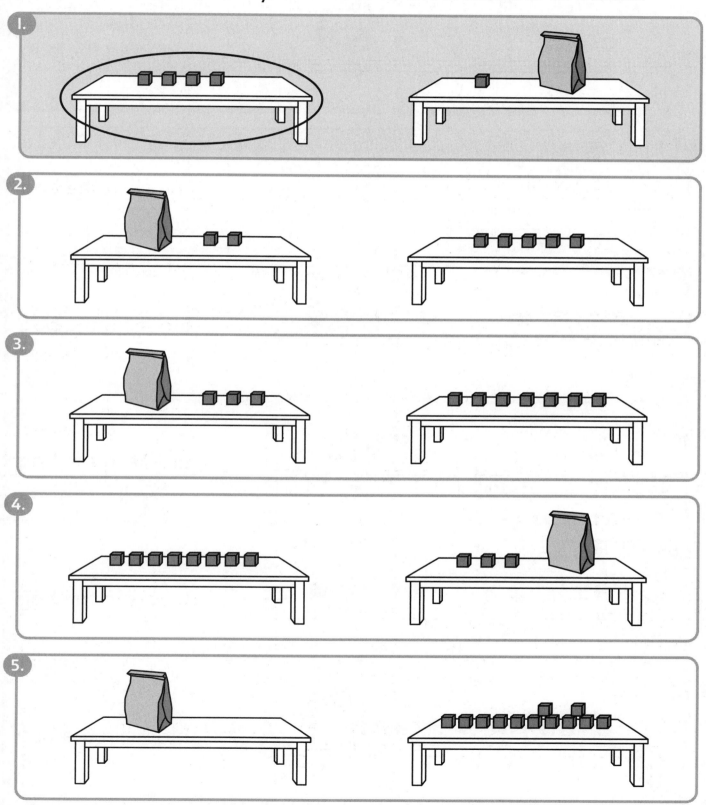

The two tables have the same number of blocks.
☐ How many blocks are in the bag?

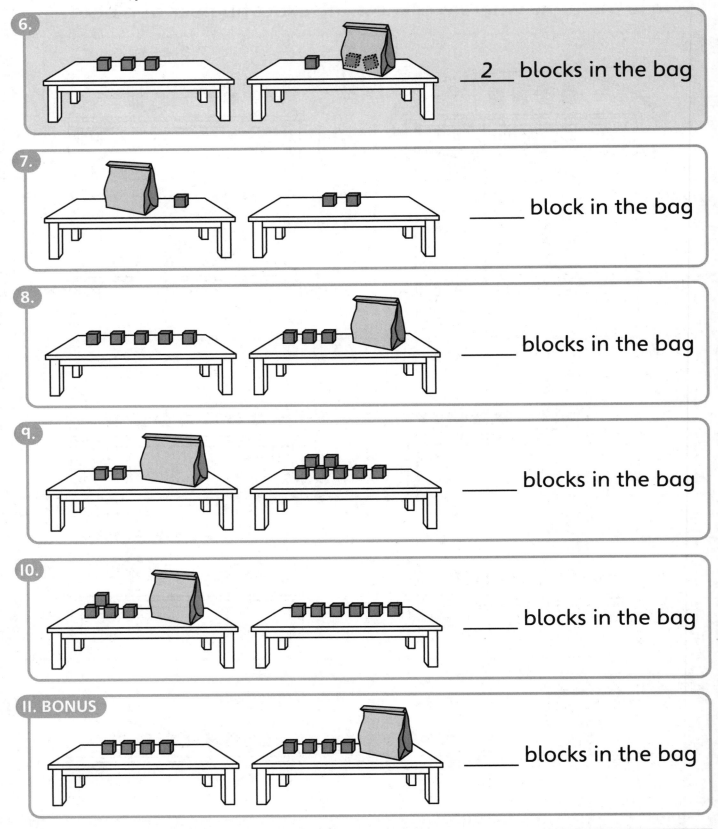

6. _2_ blocks in the bag

7. _____ block in the bag

8. _____ blocks in the bag

9. _____ blocks in the bag

10. _____ blocks in the bag

11. BONUS _____ blocks in the bag

The tables have the same number of balls.
⬭ Draw the balls that are in the box.

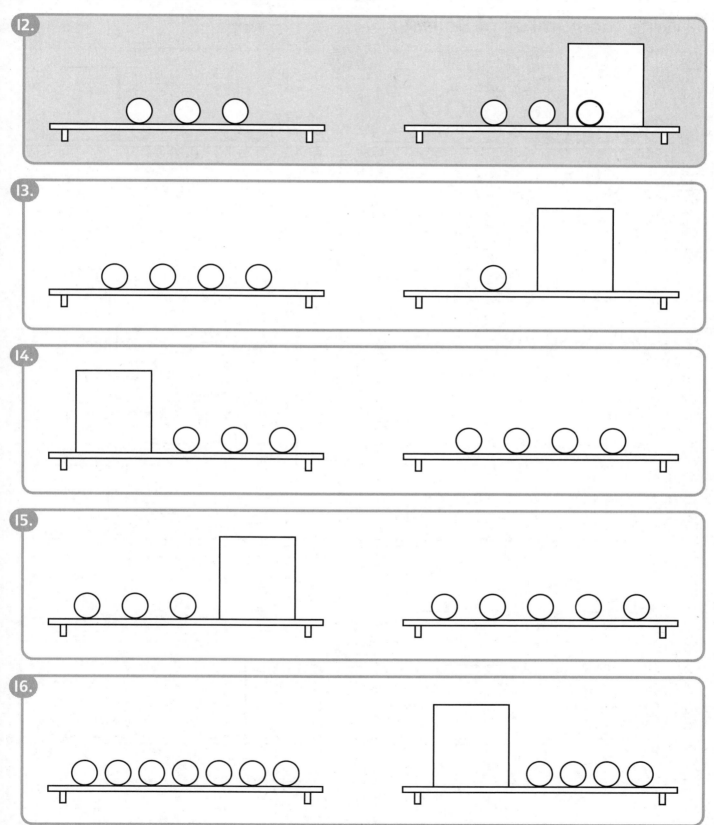

The tables have the same number of balls.
◯ Draw the balls that are in the box.
◯ Write the number of balls.

17.

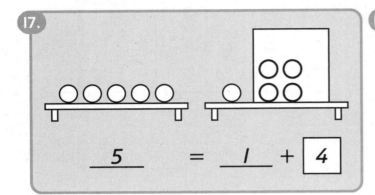

$\underline{\ \ 5\ \ } = \underline{\ \ 1\ \ } + \boxed{4}$

18.

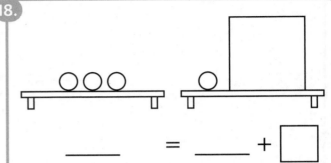

$\underline{\hspace{2em}} = \underline{\hspace{2em}} + \boxed{}$

19.

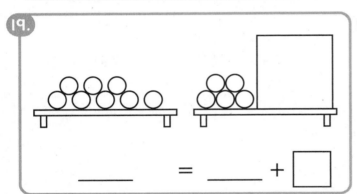

$\underline{\hspace{2em}} = \underline{\hspace{2em}} + \boxed{}$

20.

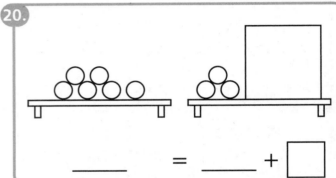

$\underline{\hspace{2em}} = \underline{\hspace{2em}} + \boxed{}$

21.

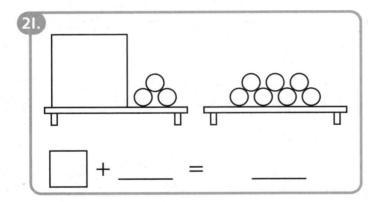

$\boxed{} + \underline{\hspace{2em}} = \underline{\hspace{2em}}$

22.

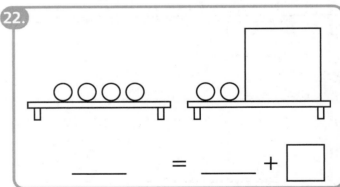

$\underline{\hspace{2em}} = \underline{\hspace{2em}} + \boxed{}$

23.

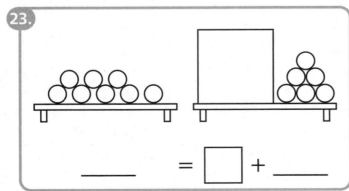

$\underline{\hspace{2em}} = \boxed{} + \underline{\hspace{2em}}$

24.

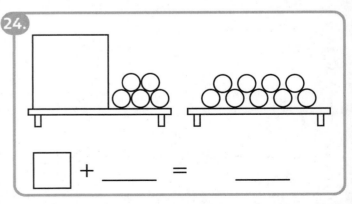

$\boxed{} + \underline{\hspace{2em}} = \underline{\hspace{2em}}$

21. Find the Missing Addend by Counting On

⬜ Write the addend you see in the ⬡.
⬜ Circle the total in the addition sentence.

1.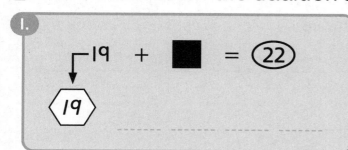

$$19 + \blacksquare = \boxed{22}$$

⟨19⟩ _____

2.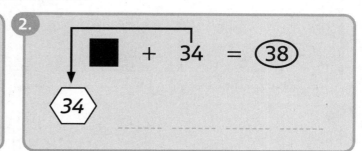

$$\blacksquare + 34 = \boxed{38}$$

⟨34⟩ _____

3.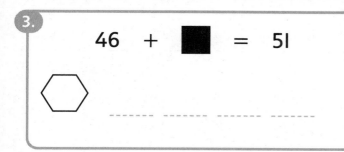

$$46 + \blacksquare = 51$$

⬡ _____

4.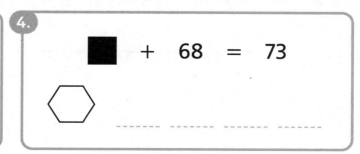

$$\blacksquare + 68 = 73$$

⬡ _____

The missing addend is the number you count on.
⬜ Find the missing addend by counting on to the total.

5.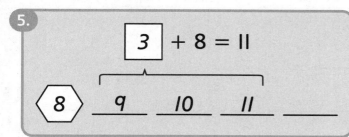

$$\boxed{3} + 8 = 11$$

⟨8⟩ 9   10   11 ____

6.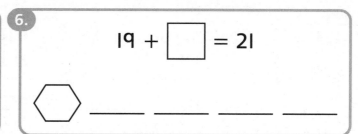

$$19 + \square = 21$$

⬡ ____ ____ ____ ____

7.

$$\square + 31 = 35$$

⬡ ____ ____ ____ ____

8.

$$48 + \square = 51$$

⬡ ____ ____ ____ ____

9.

$$73 + \square = 77$$

⬡ ____ ____ ____ ____

10.

$$\square + 86 = 90$$

⬡ ____ ____ ____ ____

⃝ Find the missing addend by counting on.

11.

$$\boxed{5} + 7 = 12$$

⬡7⟩ _8_ _9_ _10_ _11_ _12_ ___ ___ ___ ___ ___

12.

$$16 + \boxed{} = 23$$

⬡ ___ ___ ___ ___ ___ ___ ___ ___ ___ ___

13.

$$\boxed{} + 29 = 37$$

⬡ ___ ___ ___ ___ ___ ___ ___ ___ ___ ___

14.

$$48 + \boxed{} = 57$$

⬡ ___ ___ ___ ___ ___ ___ ___ ___ ___ ___

15.

$$\boxed{} + 67 = 72$$

⬡ ___ ___ ___ ___ ___ ___ ___ ___ ___ ___

16.

$$85 + \boxed{} = 94$$

⬡ ___ ___ ___ ___ ___ ___ ___ ___ ___ ___

22. Word Problems with One Addend Missing (1)

☐ Write the number sentence for the story.

1.

There are ■ red marbles.

There are 5 blue marbles.

There are 9 marbles altogether.

$$\begin{array}{r} ■ \\ +\ \ 5 \\ \hline 9 \end{array}$$

2.

There are 4 small dogs.

There are ■ large dogs.

There are 7 dogs altogether.

3.

There are 4 red cars.

There are ■ blue cars.

There are 6 cars altogether.

4.

There are ■ robins.

There are 5 owls.

There are 8 birds altogether.

5.

There are ■ picture books.

There are 2 story books.

There are 10 books altogether.

○ Write the number sentence for the story.
○ Write the missing addend.

6.

There are ⬚5⬚ children at the park.

There are 3 adults at the park.

There are 8 people altogether.

$$\begin{array}{r} \boxed{5} \\ +3 \\ \hline 8 \end{array}$$

7.

There are 7 glasses of milk.

There are ⬚ glasses of water.

There are 10 glasses altogether.

8.

Sarah has 4 stickers.

Ravi has ⬚ stickers.

Together, they have 10 stickers.

9.

Amy has ⬚ hockey cards.

Amy has 2 basketball cards.

Amy has 7 cards altogether.

10.

There are 2 open doors.

There are ⬚ closed doors.

There are 8 doors altogether.

23. Word Problems with One Addend Missing (2)

☐ Write the number sentence for the story.
☐ Write the missing addend.

1.

There were 3 rabbits on the grass.

[2] more rabbits came.

Now there are 5 rabbits on the grass.

$$
\begin{array}{r}
3 \\
+\ \boxed{2} \\
\hline
5
\end{array}
$$

2.

There were 14 toys in the box.

Sam put [ ] more toys in the box.

Now there are 17 toys in the box.

3.

Nina did 32 jumping jacks.

Then she did [ ] more jumping jacks.

Altogether, she did 36 jumping jacks.

4.

David counted 51 pens in the class.

Then he found [ ] more.

Altogether, he counted 56 pens.

5.

Tasha wrote 63 words.

Then she wrote [ ] more words.

Altogether, she wrote 68 words.

○ Write the number sentence for the story.
○ Write the missing addend.

6.

| 5 | birds flew to a tree. |

10 more birds flew to the tree.

Now there are 15 birds in the tree.

$$\begin{array}{r} 5 \\ + \;\; 10 \\ \hline 15 \end{array}$$

7.

☐ books were on the shelf.

Greg put 20 more books on the shelf.

Now there are 26 books on the shelf.

8.

☐ names were in the jar.

May put 30 more names in the jar.

Altogether, there were 37 names in the jar.

9.

Ben read ☐ pages before school.

He read 32 more pages after school.

Altogether, he read 39 pages.

10.

☐ kids went to the zoo.

Then 41 more kids went to the zoo.

Now there are 47 kids at the zoo.

11.

The team won ☐ points.

Then the team won 71 more points.

Altogether, the team won 79 points.

24. Subtract Using Addition

☐ Write two subtraction sentences.
☐ Circle the totals.

1.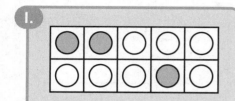

$\boxed{10} - \underline{\ 3\ } = \underline{\ 7\ }$

$\boxed{10} - \underline{\ 7\ } = \underline{\ 3\ }$

2.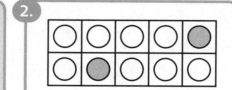

$10 - \underline{\ 2\ } = \underline{\ \ \ }$

$10 - \underline{\ 8\ } = \underline{\ \ \ }$

3.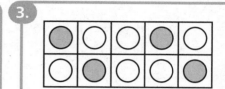

$10 - \underline{\ \ \ } = \underline{\ \ \ }$

$10 - \underline{\ \ \ } = \underline{\ \ \ }$

4.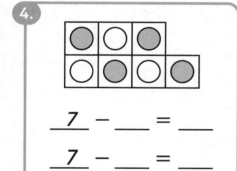

$\underline{\ 7\ } - \underline{\ \ \ } = \underline{\ \ \ }$

$\underline{\ 7\ } - \underline{\ \ \ } = \underline{\ \ \ }$

5.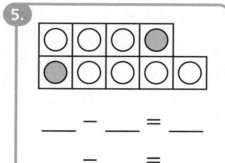

$\underline{\ \ \ } - \underline{\ \ \ } = \underline{\ \ \ }$

$\underline{\ \ \ } - \underline{\ \ \ } = \underline{\ \ \ }$

6.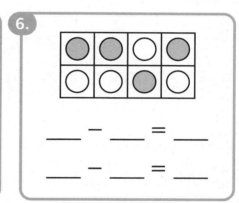

$\underline{\ \ \ } - \underline{\ \ \ } = \underline{\ \ \ }$

$\underline{\ \ \ } - \underline{\ \ \ } = \underline{\ \ \ }$

☐ Write two addition sentences.
☐ Write two subtraction sentences.
☐ Circle the totals.

7.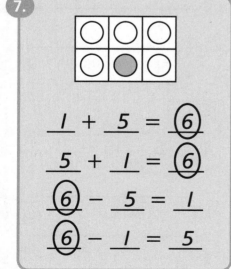

$\underline{\ 1\ } + \underline{\ 5\ } = \boxed{6}$

$\underline{\ 5\ } + \underline{\ 1\ } = \boxed{6}$

$\boxed{6} - \underline{\ 5\ } = \underline{\ 1\ }$

$\boxed{6} - \underline{\ 1\ } = \underline{\ 5\ }$

8.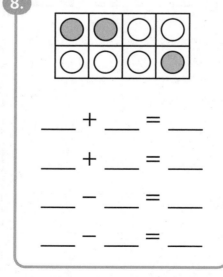

$\underline{\ \ \ } + \underline{\ \ \ } = \underline{\ \ \ }$

$\underline{\ \ \ } + \underline{\ \ \ } = \underline{\ \ \ }$

$\underline{\ \ \ } - \underline{\ \ \ } = \underline{\ \ \ }$

$\underline{\ \ \ } - \underline{\ \ \ } = \underline{\ \ \ }$

9.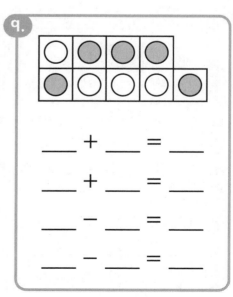

$\underline{\ \ \ } + \underline{\ \ \ } = \underline{\ \ \ }$

$\underline{\ \ \ } + \underline{\ \ \ } = \underline{\ \ \ }$

$\underline{\ \ \ } - \underline{\ \ \ } = \underline{\ \ \ }$

$\underline{\ \ \ } - \underline{\ \ \ } = \underline{\ \ \ }$

☐ Circle the total.

☐ Write two subtraction sentences for the addition.

10.

$3 + 7 = \boxed{10}$

$\underline{10 - 3 = 7}$

$\underline{10 - 7 = 3}$

11.

$2 + 5 = \boxed{7}$

$\underline{7 - 2 = 5}$

$\underline{\hspace{3cm}}$

12.

$3 + 6 = \boxed{9}$

$\underline{\hspace{3cm}}$

$\underline{\hspace{3cm}}$

13.

$9 + 2 = 11$

$\underline{\hspace{3cm}}$

$\underline{\hspace{3cm}}$

14.

$12 = 5 + 7$

$\underline{\hspace{3cm}}$

$\underline{\hspace{3cm}}$

15.

$13 = 4 + 9$

$\underline{\hspace{3cm}}$

$\underline{\hspace{3cm}}$

☐ Circle the total.

☐ Write two addition sentences for the subtraction.

16.

$\boxed{8} - 3 = 5$

$\underline{3 + 5 = 8}$

$\underline{5 + 3 = 8}$

17.

$\boxed{12} - 4 = 8$

$\underline{4 + 8 = 12}$

$\underline{\hspace{3cm}}$

18.

$\boxed{7} - 3 = 4$

$\underline{\hspace{3cm}}$

$\underline{\hspace{3cm}}$

19.

$11 - 6 = 5$

$\underline{\hspace{3cm}}$

$\underline{\hspace{3cm}}$

20.

$7 = 9 - 2$

$\underline{\hspace{3cm}}$

$\underline{\hspace{3cm}}$

21.

$8 = 15 - 7$

$\underline{\hspace{3cm}}$

$\underline{\hspace{3cm}}$

JUMP Math Accumula

$$1 + 6 = 7 \qquad 1 + 7 = 8 \qquad 1 + 8 = 9$$
$$2 + 5 = 7 \qquad 2 + 6 = 8 \qquad 2 + 7 = 9$$
$$3 + 4 = 7 \qquad 3 + 5 = 8 \qquad 3 + 6 = 9$$
$$\qquad\qquad\quad 4 + 4 = 8 \qquad 4 + 5 = 9$$

☐ Which fact do you use?

22.
$$7 - 2$$
Use $2 + \underline{\ 5\ } = 7$

23.
$$8 - 1$$
Use $1 + \underline{\qquad} = 8$

24.
$$9 - 3$$
Use $3 + \underline{\qquad} = 9$

25.
$$9 - 5$$
Use $\underline{\ 4\ } + 5 = 9$

26.
$$7 - 6$$
Use $\underline{\qquad} + 6 = 7$

27.
$$8 - 5$$
Use $\underline{\qquad} + 5 = 8$

☐ Use an addition fact to subtract.

28.
$$7 - 2$$
$2 + \underline{\ 5\ } = 7$
So $7 - 2 = \underline{\ 5\ }$

29.
$$8 - 6$$
$6 + \underline{\ 2\ } = 8$
So $8 - 6 = \underline{\qquad}$

30.
$$7 - 4$$
$4 + \underline{\qquad} = 7$
So $7 - 4 = \underline{\qquad}$

31.
$$9 - 2$$
$2 + \underline{\qquad} = 9$
So $9 - 2 = \underline{\qquad}$

32.
$$8 - 4$$
$4 + \underline{\qquad} = 8$
So $8 - 4 = \underline{\qquad}$

33.
$$10 - 2$$
$2 + \underline{\qquad} = 10$
So $10 - 2 = \underline{\qquad}$

34.
$$10 - 4 \qquad 8 - 3 \qquad 9 - 4 \qquad 6 - 1 \qquad 12 - 8 \qquad 11 - 9$$

25. Subtract by Counting On

Will wants to find 6 − 2 = ___. He counts on to solve 2 + ___ = 6.

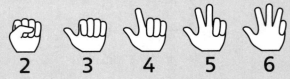

2   3   4   5   6

The answer is the number of fingers. So 6 − 2 = _4_ .

⬜ Find the missing number by counting on.

1.
7 − 5 = _2_

5 + _2_ = 7

2.
5 − 4 = ___

4 + ___ = 5

3.
5 − 3 = ___

3 + ___ = 5

4.
9 − 2 = ___

2 + ___ = 9

5.
11 − 8 = _3_

8 + _3_ = 11

6.
12 − 7 = ___

7 + ___ = 12

7.
15 − 13 = ___

13 + ___ = 15

8.
27 − 22 = ___

22 + ___ = 27

9.
12 − 9 = ___

9 + ___ = 12

10.
7 − 4 = ___

4 + ___ = 7

11.
8 − 6 = ___

6 + ___ = 8

12.
15 − 11 = ___

11 + ___ = 15

⬜ Subtract.

13.
9 − 7 = ___

14.
5 − 2 = ___

15.
12 − 8 = ___

16.
11 − 4 = ___

17.
6 − 5 = ___

18.
8 − 5 = ___

19.
14 − 12 = ___

20.
26 − 23 = ___

21.
17 − 11 = ___

22.
35 − 33 = ___

23.
19 − 16 = ___

24.
15 − 9 = ___

26. Compare Using Subtraction

☐ Use the word sentence to subtract.

1.
6 is **2** more than 4.

6 − 4 = __2__

2.
5 is **3** more than 2.

5 − 2 = _____

3.
15 is **7** more than 8.

15 − 8 = _____

4.
95 is **12** more than 83.

95 − 83 = _____

☐ Subtract.

5.
7 is how many more than 5?

__7__ − __5__ = _____

6.
8 is how many more than 3?

__8__ − _____ = _____

7.
13 is how many more than 9?

_____ − _____ = _____

8.
5 is how many more than 3?

_____ − _____ = _____

9.
17 is how many more than 14?

_____ − _____ = _____

10.
16 is how many more than 2?

_____ − _____ = _____

11.
9 is how many more than 6?

_____ − _____ = _____

12.
13 is how many more than 3?

_____ − _____ = _____

13. BONUS
25 is how many more than 21?

14. BONUS
36 is how many more than 29?

☐ Write the subtraction.

15.

Sara has 7 apples. Anna has 5 apples.

Sara has ___7 – 5___ more apples.

16.

Marco has 6 crayons. Amit has 4 crayons.

Marco has ___6 –___ more crayons.

17.

Rani has 12 marbles. Jayden has 10 marbles.

Rani has _____ more marbles.

☐ Write the subtraction.
☐ Subtract.

18.

Kate has 7 stamps. Ben has 5 stamps.

How many more stamps does Kate have?

___7 – 5___ = __2__

19.

Lily has 9 stickers. Peter has 6 stickers.

How many more stickers does Lily have?

___9 –___ = _____

20.

Tom has 17 balloons. Zara has 7 balloons.

How many more balloons does Tom have?

_____ = _____

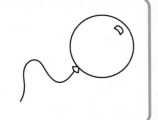

27. Missing Numbers in Subtraction

☐ Write the total number of boxes.
☐ Write two subtraction sentences.

1.
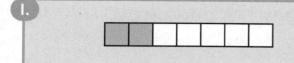

Total ___7___

___7___ – ___2___ = ___5___

___7___ – ___5___ = ___2___

2.

Total ___5___

___5___ – ___1___ = ___4___

_____ – _____ = _____

3.

Total _____

_____ – _____ = _____

_____ – _____ = _____

4.

Total _____

_____ – _____ = _____

_____ – _____ = _____

To find 8 – ☐ = 5, use 8 – ___5___ = ☐3☐. So 8 – ☐3☐ = 5.

☐ Find the missing numbers.

5.

8 – ☐3☐ = 5

8 – ___5___ = ☐3☐

6.

6 – ☐ = 4

6 – _____ = ☐

7.

7 – ☐ = 4

7 – _____ = ☐

8.

12 – ☐ = 8

12 – _____ = ☐

9.

9 – ☐ = 3

9 – _____ = ☐

10.

10 – ☐ = 6

10 – _____ = ☐

☐ Color the answer.

11. 8 bunnies were eating grass. Some hopped away.
6 bunnies kept eating. How many hopped away?

12. 6 fish swam in a pond. Some swam away.
2 fish stayed in the pond. How many swam away?

13. 5 cats were playing. Some took a nap.
1 cat kept playing. How many took a nap?

14. 7 ants marched up a wall. Some fell down.
3 ants were left. How many fell down?

15. 6 pears were on a plate. Alice ate some.
3 pears were left. How many did Alice eat?

JUMP Math Accumula

28. Missing Total in Subtraction

☐ Draw the dots on the big domino.
☐ Write the total.

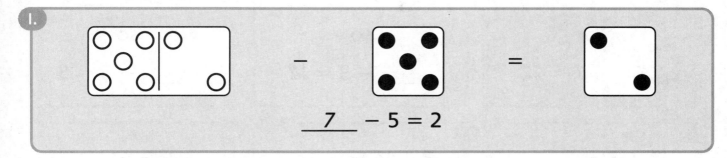

1. $\underline{7} - 5 = 2$

2. $\underline{} - 3 = 4$

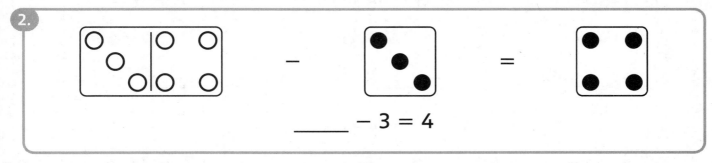

3. $\underline{} - 4 = 6$

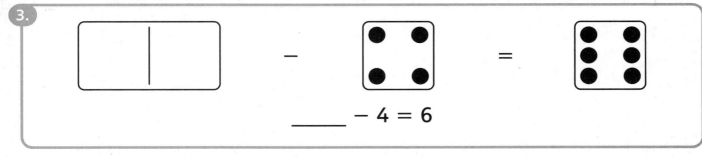

4. $\underline{} - 7 = 4$

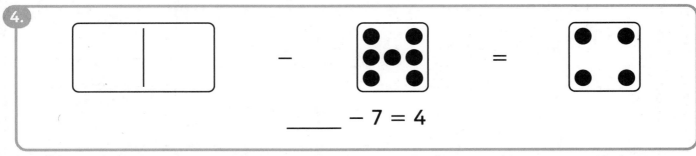

5. $\underline{} - 9 = 6$

⬭ Find the missing total.

6.
$$12 + 4 = \underline{\,16\,}$$
so
$$\underline{\,16\,} - 4 = 12$$

7.
$$14 + 3 = \underline{\quad}$$
so
$$\underline{\quad} - 3 = 14$$

8.
$$5 + 5 = \underline{\quad}$$
so
$$\underline{\quad} - 5 = 5$$

9.
$$12 + 5 = \underline{\quad}$$
so
$$\underline{\quad} - 5 = 12$$

10.
$$3 + 14 = \underline{\quad}$$
so
$$\underline{\quad} - 14 = 3$$

11.
$$7 + 6 = \underline{\quad}$$
so
$$\underline{\quad} - 6 = 7$$

12.
$$27 + 4 = \underline{\quad}$$
so
$$\underline{\quad} - 4 = 27$$

13.
$$36 + 3 = \underline{\quad}$$
so
$$\underline{\quad} - 3 = 36$$

14.
$$2 + 25 = \underline{\quad}$$
so
$$\underline{\quad} - 25 = 2$$

⬭ Find the missing total.

15.

$\underline{\quad} - 3 = 5$	$\underline{\quad} - 2 = 8$	$\underline{\quad} - 2 = 7$
$\underline{\quad} - 4 = 15$	$\underline{\quad} - 5 = 6$	$\underline{\quad} - 22 = 5$
$\underline{\quad} - 2 = 32$	$\underline{\quad} - 26 = 3$	$\underline{\quad} - 6 = 7$
$\underline{\quad} - 45 = 2$	$\underline{\quad} - 2 = 56$	$\underline{\quad} - 78 = 1$
$\underline{\quad} - 64 = 3$	$\underline{\quad} - 5 = 39$	$\underline{\quad} - 82 = 2$

29. Subtraction Word Problems

◯ Write a number sentence for the story.
◯ Find the missing number.

1.

There were $\boxed{8}$ apples in the tree.

3 apples fell down.

Now there are 5 apples in the tree.

$$\begin{array}{r} \boxed{8} \\ -3 \\ \hline 5 \end{array}$$

2.

There were $\boxed{}$ rabbits on the grass.

5 rabbits hopped away.

Now there are 2 rabbits on the grass.

3.

There were $\boxed{}$ books on the shelf.

Miss Chen took 4 books.

Now there are 7 books on the shelf.

4.

Nina had 10 raisins.

She ate $\boxed{}$ raisins.

Nina has 6 raisins left.

$$\begin{array}{r} 10 \\ -\boxed{} \\ \hline 6 \end{array}$$

5.

There were 9 toys in the toy box.

Roy took out $\boxed{}$ toys.

Now there are 6 toys in the toy box.

⬜ Write the number sentence for the story.
⬜ Write the answer.

6.
Ravi had **8** berries.
He ate some berries.
Now Ravi has 3 berries left.
How many berries did he eat? ___5___

$$\begin{array}{r} 8 \\ -\ 5 \\ \hline 3 \end{array}$$

7.
Kim had **9** books.
She gave some away.
Now she has 7 books.
How many books did Kim give away? _____

8.
There were 8 apples in the tree.
Some apples fell.
Now there are 2 apples in the tree.
How many apples fell? _____

9.
There were some birds in a tree.
Then 5 birds flew away.
Now there are 2 birds in the tree.
How many birds were in the tree before? _____

10.
There were some frogs in the pond.
Then 3 frogs hopped out.
Now there are 6 frogs in the pond.
How many frogs were in the pond before? _____

30. Tens and Ones Blocks

◻ What number do the ones show?

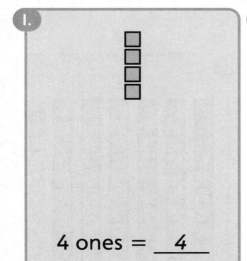

1. 4 ones = __4__

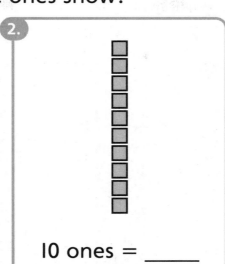

2. 10 ones = _____

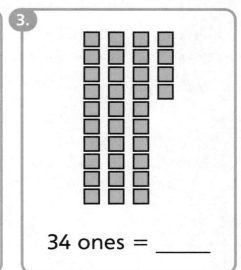

3. 34 ones = _____

◻ Write the number of tens.

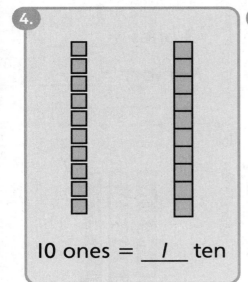

4. 10 ones = __1__ ten

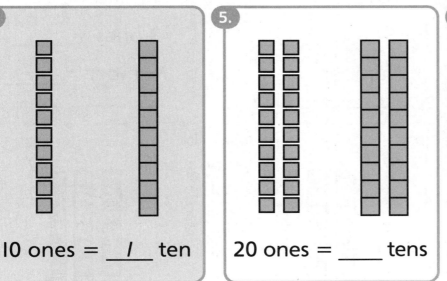

5. 20 ones = _____ tens

6. 30 ones = _____ tens

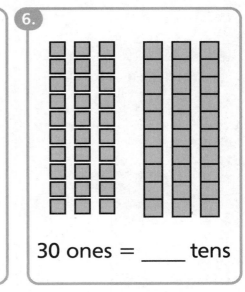

◻ Write the number.

7. 4 tens = __40__

8. 6 tens = _____

9. 8 tens = _____

10 9 tens = _____

11. 7 tens = _____

12. 5 tens = _____

○ What number do the tens show?
○ What number do the ones show?
○ What is the number?

13.

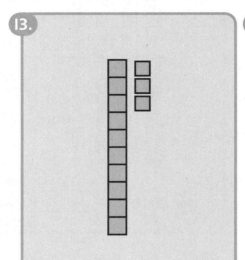

1 ten = _10_

3 ones = _3_

Number = _13_

14.

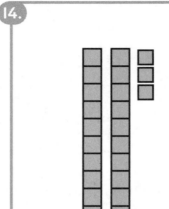

2 tens = _____

3 ones = _____

Number = _____

15.

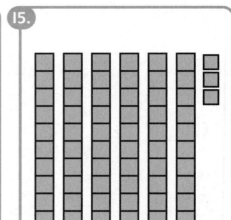

6 tens = _____

3 ones = _____

Number = _____

16.

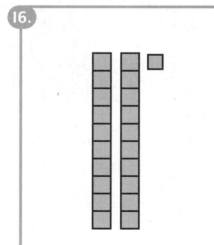

2 tens = _____

1 one = _____

Number = _____

17.

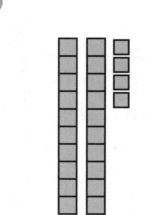

2 tens = _____

4 ones = _____

Number = _____

18.

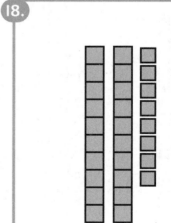

2 tens = _____

8 ones = _____

Number = _____

☐ Use the number of tens and ones to write the number.

19.
3 tens = _30_

8 ones = _8_

Number = _38_

20.
5 tens = _____

7 ones = _____

Number = _____

21.
9 tens = _____

2 ones = _____

Number = _____

22.
6 tens and 1 one = _61_

23.
5 tens and 4 ones = _____

24.
2 tens and 2 ones = _____

25.
7 tens and 3 ones = _____

☐ Circle ones and tens to show the number.

26.
53
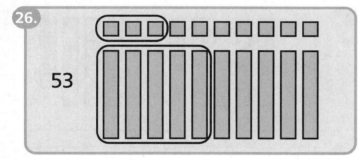

27.
15

28.
68
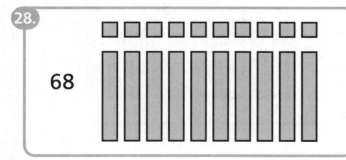

29.
72
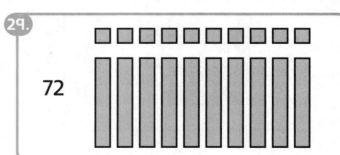

30.
81
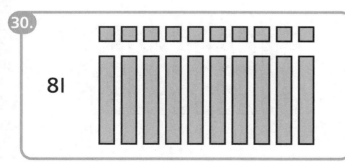

31.
97
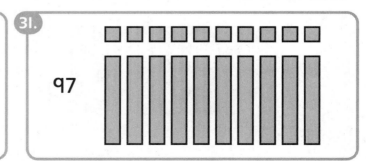

◯ Draw tens (|) and ones (•) to show the number.

32. 23 | | :
  •

33. 17

34. 32

35. 46

36. 51

37. 75

◯ Circle the picture that shows the number.

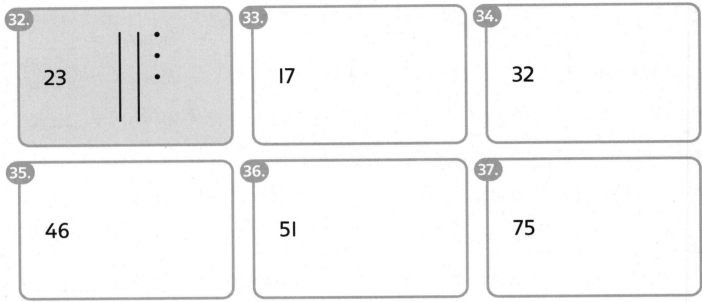

38. 12

39. 34

40. 23

41. 41

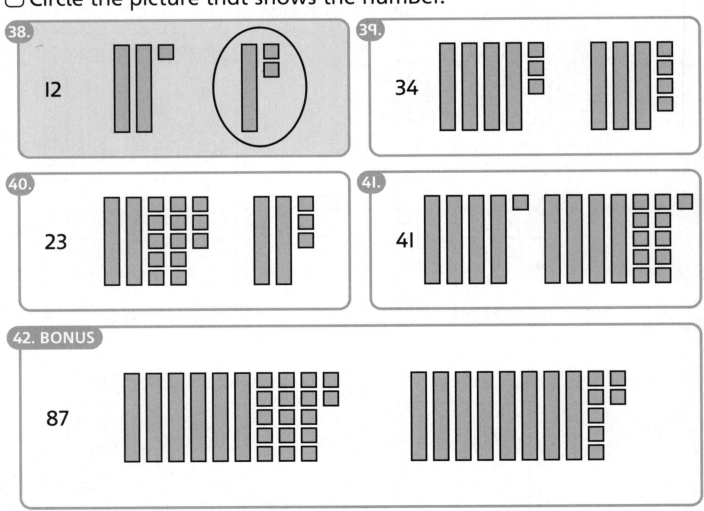

42. BONUS

87

○ Circle the picture that does **not** show the number.

43. 42

44. 56

45. 33

46. 67

47. 28

48. 71

31. Adding a 1-Digit Number to a 2-Digit Number

☐ Count on to add.

1.

$45 + 3 = \underline{\ \ ?\ \ }$ 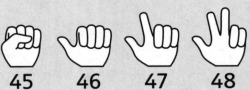 $45 + 3 = \underline{\ \ 48\ \ }$

45   46   47   48

2.

$16 + 2 = \underline{\quad}$ $16 + 4 = \underline{\quad}$ $16 + 7 = \underline{\quad}$

3.

$26 + 2 = \underline{\quad}$ $36 + 4 = \underline{\quad}$ $46 + 7 = \underline{\quad}$

4.

$56 + 2 = \underline{\quad}$ $56 + 4 = \underline{\quad}$ $56 + 7 = \underline{\quad}$

5.

$86 + 2 = \underline{\quad}$ $86 + 4 = \underline{\quad}$ $86 + 7 = \underline{\quad}$

6.

$34 + 4 = \underline{\quad}$ $34 + 6 = \underline{\quad}$ $34 + 9 = \underline{\quad}$

7.

$64 + 4 = \underline{\quad}$ $64 + 6 = \underline{\quad}$ $64 + 9 = \underline{\quad}$

8.

$74 + 4 = \underline{\quad}$ $74 + 6 = \underline{\quad}$ $74 + 9 = \underline{\quad}$

☐ Count on to add.

9.

$48 + 1 = \underline{\hspace{2cm}}$ $58 + 1 = \underline{\hspace{2cm}}$ $68 + 1 = \underline{\hspace{2cm}}$

10.

$48 + 2 = \underline{\hspace{2cm}}$ $58 + 2 = \underline{\hspace{2cm}}$ $68 + 2 = \underline{\hspace{2cm}}$

11.

$48 + 3 = \underline{\hspace{2cm}}$ $58 + 3 = \underline{\hspace{2cm}}$ $68 + 3 = \underline{\hspace{2cm}}$

12.

$57 + 2 = \underline{\hspace{2cm}}$ $67 + 2 = \underline{\hspace{2cm}}$ $77 + 2 = \underline{\hspace{2cm}}$

13.

$57 + 3 = \underline{\hspace{2cm}}$ $67 + 3 = \underline{\hspace{2cm}}$ $77 + 3 = \underline{\hspace{2cm}}$

14.

$57 + 5 = \underline{\hspace{2cm}}$ $67 + 5 = \underline{\hspace{2cm}}$ $77 + 5 = \underline{\hspace{2cm}}$

15.

$65 + 4 = \underline{\hspace{2cm}}$ $75 + 4 = \underline{\hspace{2cm}}$ $85 + 4 = \underline{\hspace{2cm}}$

16.

$65 + 5 = \underline{\hspace{2cm}}$ $75 + 5 = \underline{\hspace{2cm}}$ $85 + 5 = \underline{\hspace{2cm}}$

17.

$65 + 9 = \underline{\hspace{2cm}}$ $75 + 9 = \underline{\hspace{2cm}}$ $85 + 9 = \underline{\hspace{2cm}}$

32. Counting by Tens

These numbers are **multiples of 10**.

10, 20, 30, 40, 50, 60, 70, 80, 90

☐ Fill in the missing multiples of 10.

1. 10, _20_, _30_, _40_, 50

2. 40, _____, _____, _____, 80

3. 40, _____, _____, _____, _____, 90

4. 20, _____, _____, _____, _____, 70

5. 10, _____, _____, _____, _____, _____, _____, _____, 90

☐ Circle the multiples of 10.

6. 48, 49, ⓢ50, 51, 52, 53, 54

7. 85, 86, 87, 88, 89, 90, 91

8. 17, 18, 19, 20, 21, 22, 23, 24, 25, 26, 27, 28, 29, 30, 31, 32

☐ Circle the next multiple of 10.

9. 12 10, ⓢ20, 30, 40

10. 38 40, 50, 60, 70

11. 79 50, 60, 70, 80

12. 45 30, 40, 50, 60

13. 67 60, 70, 80, 90

14. 53 30, 40, 50, 60

33. Using Base Ten Blocks to Add (No Regrouping)

⬭ Write the number of tens and ones the addition makes.
⬭ Add.

1.
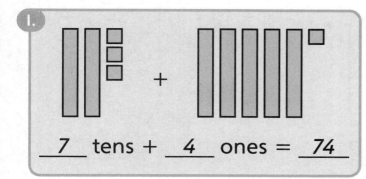

__7__ tens + __4__ ones = __74__

2.
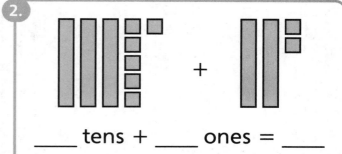

____ tens + ____ ones = ____

3.
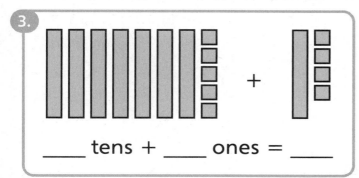

____ tens + ____ ones = ____

4.
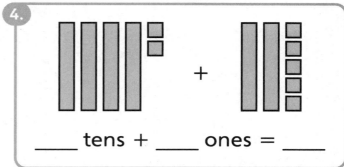

____ tens + ____ ones = ____

⬭ Write the numbers that the blocks show.
⬭ Use the blocks to help add.

5.

__15__ + __21__ = __36__

6.
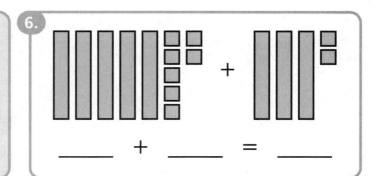

____ + ____ = ____

7.
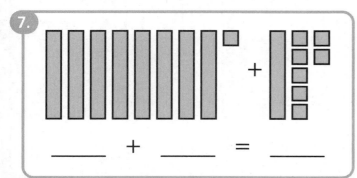

____ + ____ = ____

8.
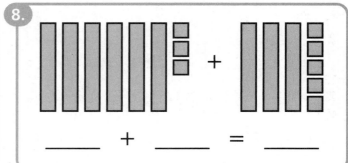

____ + ____ = ____

Draw tens and ones to show the numbers.
Use the drawings to help add.

9.

17   +   32   =   _49_

10.

25   +   41   =   ____

11.

54   +   35   =   ____

12.

72   +   16   =   ____

34. Making 10 to Add (1-Digit to 2-Digit)

☐ Add to make 10.

1. $8 + \underline{\ 2\ } = 10$

2. $7 + \underline{\quad} = 10$

3. $5 + \underline{\quad} = 10$

4. $6 + \underline{\quad} = 10$

5. $1 + \underline{\quad} = 10$

6. $4 + \underline{\quad} = 10$

7. $3 + \underline{\quad} = 10$

8. $2 + \underline{\quad} = 10$

☐ Add to make the next multiple of 10.

9. $7 + \underline{\ 3\ } = 10$ $\qquad 47 + \underline{\ 3\ } = 50 \qquad 87 + \underline{\ 3\ } = 90$

10. $2 + \underline{\quad} = 10 \qquad 32 + \underline{\quad} = 40 \qquad 72 + \underline{\quad} = 80$

11. $6 + \underline{\quad} = 10 \qquad 26 + \underline{\quad} = 30 \qquad 56 + \underline{\quad} = 60$

12. $1 + \underline{\quad} = 10 \qquad 11 + \underline{\quad} = 20 \qquad 61 + \underline{\quad} = 70$

☐ Add to make the next multiple of 10.

13. $28 + \underline{\ 2\ } = 30$

14. $34 + \underline{\quad} = 40$

15. $49 + \underline{\quad} = 50$

16. $21 + \underline{\quad} = 30$

17. $67 + \underline{\quad} = 70$

18. $52 + \underline{\quad} = 60$

19. $75 + \underline{\quad} = 80$

20. $86 + \underline{\quad} = 90$

21. $33 + \underline{\quad} = 40$

○ Fill in the blank so that the first two numbers add to 10.

22.
8 + 5

8 + __2__ + 3

23.
6 + 9

6 + ____ + 5

24.
3 + 9

3 + ____ + 2

25.
7 + 8

7 + ____ + 5

26.
9 + 4

9 + ____ + 3

27.
5 + 7

5 + ____ + 2

28.
4 + 8

4 + ____ + 2

29.
9 + 9

9 + ____ + 8

○ Circle the one that is easiest to add.

30.

34 + 7

34 + 2 + 5

34 + 7

34 + 6 + 1

34 + 7

34 + 3 + 4

31.

85 + 9

85 + 8 + 1

85 + 9

85 + 3 + 6

85 + 9

85 + 5 + 4

32.

67 + 8

67 + 3 + 5

67 + 8

67 + 7 + 1

67 + 8

67 + 2 + 6

82

JUMP Math Accumula

Fill in the blanks so that the first two numbers add to a multiple of 10.

33.

17 + 4

17 + _3_ + _1_

17 + 5

17 + ___ + ___

17 + 8

17 + ___ + ___

34.

24 + 7

24 + ___ + ___

24 + 8

24 + ___ + ___

24 + 9

24 + ___ + ___

35.

58 + 3

58 + ___ + ___

58 + 6

58 + ___ + ___

58 + 8

58 + ___ + ___

36.

78 + 5

78 + _2_ + _3_

37.

26 + 9

26 + ___ + ___

38.

35 + 6

35 + ___ + ___

39.

67 + 4

67 + ___ + ___

40.

38 + 5

38 + ___ + ___

41.

59 + 3

59 + ___ + ___

42.

29 + 7

29 + ___ + ___

43.

43 + 8

43 + ___ + ___

44.

76 + 6

76 + ___ + ___

Fill in the blanks so that the first two numbers add to a multiple of 10.

Add to make the next multiple of 10.

45.
53 + 8

53 + _7_ + _1_

_60_ + _1_

46.
29 + 3

29 + ___ + ___

___ + ___

47.
37 + 6

37 + ___ + ___

___ + ___

48.
18 + 5

18 + ___ + ___

___ + ___

49.
77 + 4

77 + ___ + ___

___ + ___

50.
86 + 9

86 + ___ + ___

___ + ___

Add.

51.
29 + 7

29 + _1_ + _6_

_30_ + _6_

_36_

52.
36 + 6

36 + ___ + ___

___ + ___

___

53.
14 + 8

14 + ___ + ___

___ + ___

___

54.
73 + 9

73 + ___ + ___

___ + ___

___

55.
44 + 8

44 + ___ + ___

___ + ___

___

56.
85 + 9

85 + ___ + ___

___ + ___

___

JUMP Math Accumula

35. Making 10 to Add (2-Digit to 2-Digit)

☐ Add.

1.
$2 + 3 = \underline{}5\underline{}$

$20 + 30 = \underline{}50\underline{}$

2.
$1 + 5 = \underline{}$

$10 + 50 = \underline{}$

3.
$3 + 4 = \underline{}$

$30 + 40 = \underline{}$

4.
$5 + 1 + 1 + 1 = \underline{}$

$50 + 10 + 10 + 10 = \underline{}$

5.
$2 + 3 + 2 + 1 = \underline{}$

$20 + 30 + 20 + 10 = \underline{}$

☐ Write the second number in expanded form.

6.
$30 + 15$

$= 30 + \underline{}10\underline{} + \underline{}5\underline{}$

7.
$50 + 19$

$= 50 + \underline{} + \underline{}$

8.
$40 + 17$

$= 40 + \underline{} + \underline{}$

☐ Write the second number in expanded form.
☐ Add the tens.

9.
$60 + 11$

$= 60 + \underline{}10\underline{} + \underline{}1\underline{}$

$= \underline{}70\underline{} + \underline{}1\underline{}$

10.
$70 + 13$

$= 70 + \underline{} + \underline{}$

$= \underline{} + \underline{}$

11.
$80 + 14$

$= 80 + \underline{} + \underline{}$

$= \underline{} + \underline{}$

☐ Write the second number in expanded form.
☐ Add the tens and ones.

12.
$20 + 14$

$= 20 + \underline{}10\underline{} + \underline{}4\underline{}$

$= \underline{}30\underline{} + \underline{}4\underline{}$

$= \underline{}34\underline{}$

13.
$50 + 18$

$= 50 + \underline{} + \underline{}$

$= \underline{} + \underline{}$

$= \underline{}$

14.
$70 + 12$

$= 70 + \underline{} + \underline{}$

$= \underline{} + \underline{}$

$= \underline{}$

☐ Add by separating the tens and ones.

15.
$$23 = 20 + 3$$
$$+\ 34 = 30 + 4$$
$$\boxed{57} \leftarrow 50 + 7$$

16.
$$34 = 30 + 4$$
$$+\ 15 = 10 + 5$$
$$\boxed{} \leftarrow 40 + 9$$

17.
$$27 = 20 + \boxed{}$$
$$+\ 22 = 20 + \boxed{}$$
$$\boxed{} \leftarrow 40 + \boxed{}$$

18.
$$35 = \boxed{} + \boxed{}$$
$$+\ 42 = \boxed{} + \boxed{}$$
$$\boxed{} \leftarrow \boxed{} + \boxed{}$$

19.
$$15 = \boxed{} + \boxed{}$$
$$+\ 23 = \boxed{} + \boxed{}$$
$$\boxed{} \leftarrow \boxed{} + \boxed{}$$

20.
$$26 = \boxed{} + \boxed{}$$
$$+\ 13 = \boxed{} + \boxed{}$$
$$\boxed{} \leftarrow \boxed{} + \boxed{}$$

21.
$$34 = \boxed{} + \boxed{}$$
$$+\ 54 = \boxed{} + \boxed{}$$
$$\boxed{} \leftarrow \boxed{} + \boxed{}$$

22.
$$26 = \boxed{} + \boxed{}$$
$$+\ 33 = \boxed{} + \boxed{}$$
$$\boxed{} \leftarrow \boxed{} + \boxed{}$$

23.
$$34 = \boxed{} + \boxed{}$$
$$13 = \boxed{} + \boxed{}$$
$$+\ 52 = \boxed{} + \boxed{}$$
$$\boxed{} \leftarrow \boxed{} + \boxed{}$$

24.
$$17 = \boxed{} + \boxed{}$$
$$20 = \boxed{} + \boxed{}$$
$$+\ 61 = \boxed{} + \boxed{}$$
$$\boxed{} \leftarrow \boxed{} + \boxed{}$$

○ Add by using a tens and ones chart.

25.

$$\begin{array}{r} 35 \\ +\ 32 \\ \hline 67 \end{array}$$

←

Tens	Ones
3	5
3	2
6	7

26.

$$\begin{array}{r} 24 \\ +\ 41 \\ \hline \end{array}$$

←

Tens	Ones
2	4
4	1

27.

$$\begin{array}{r} 46 \\ +\ 31 \\ \hline \end{array}$$

←

Tens	Ones

28.

$$\begin{array}{r} 43 \\ +\ 23 \\ \hline \end{array}$$

←

Tens	Ones

29.

$$\begin{array}{r} 27 \\ +\ 21 \\ +\ 51 \\ \hline \end{array}$$

←

Tens	Ones

30.

$$\begin{array}{r} 31 \\ +\ 42 \\ +\ 14 \\ \hline \end{array}$$

←

Tens	Ones

31. BONUS

$$\begin{array}{r} 37 \\ +\ 22 \\ \hline \end{array} \qquad \begin{array}{r} 63 \\ +\ 16 \\ \hline \end{array} \qquad \begin{array}{r} 25 \\ +\ 34 \\ \hline \end{array} \qquad \begin{array}{r} 31 \\ +\ 62 \\ \hline \end{array} \qquad \begin{array}{r} 54 \\ +\ 34 \\ \hline \end{array} \qquad \begin{array}{r} 23 \\ +\ 43 \\ \hline \end{array}$$

32.

Clara collects stickers. She has
16 bird stickers and 22 animal stickers.
How many stickers does Clara have?

◯ Circle 10 ones to make a ten.
◯ **Regroup** in the next row.

33.

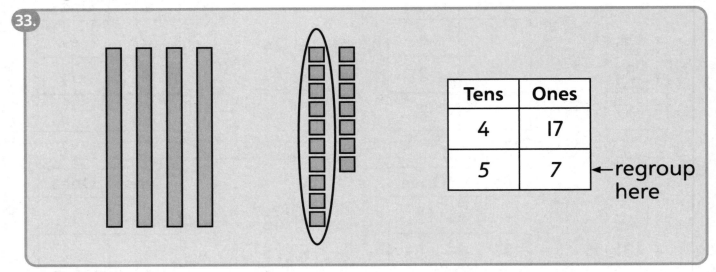

Tens	Ones
4	17
5	7	← regroup here

34.

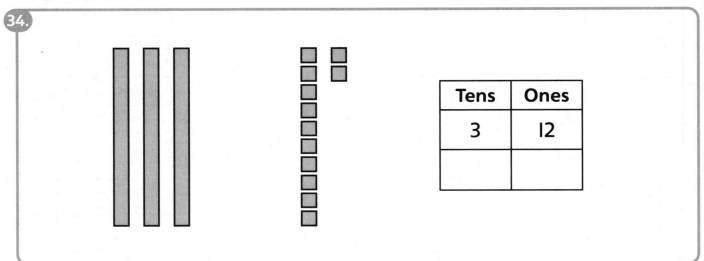

Tens	Ones
3	12

35.

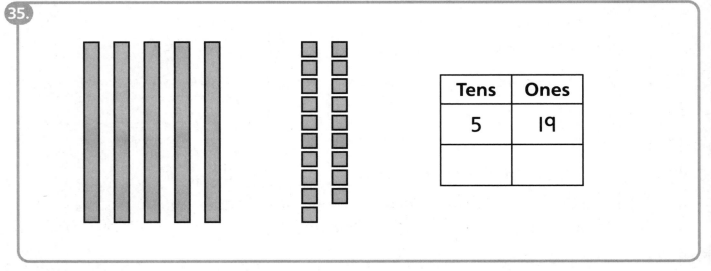

Tens	Ones
5	19

JUMP Math Accumula

☐ Circle 10 ones to make a ten.
☐ **Regroup** in the next row.

36.

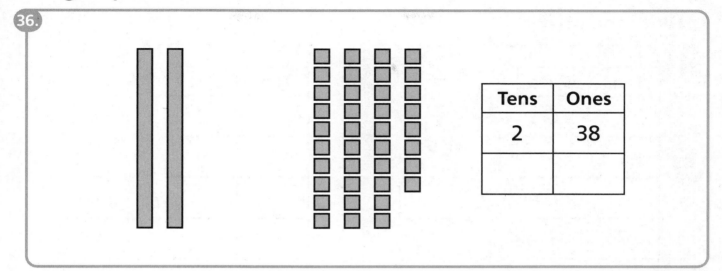

Tens	Ones
2	38

37.

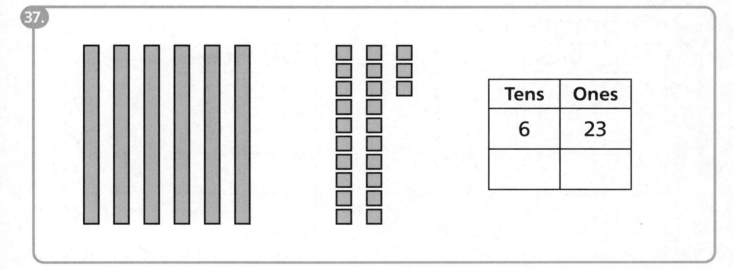

Tens	Ones
6	23

☐ Regroup in the next row.

38.

Tens	Ones
5	31

39.

Tens	Ones
7	25

40.

Tens	Ones
6	24

☐ Add the tens and the ones.
☐ Regroup in the next row.
☐ Write the answer.

41.

Tens	Ones
1	6
5	5
6	11
7	1

$$\begin{array}{r} 16 \\ + \ 55 \\ \hline \boxed{71} \end{array}$$

42.

Tens	Ones
1	2
2	9

$$\begin{array}{r} 12 \\ + \ 29 \\ \hline \ \end{array}$$

43.

Tens	Ones
2	5
3	8

$$\begin{array}{r} 25 \\ + \ 38 \\ \hline \ \end{array}$$

44.

Tens	Ones
5	7
2	6

$$\begin{array}{r} 57 \\ + \ 26 \\ \hline \ \end{array}$$

45.

Tens	Ones
1	6
3	4
2	8

$$\begin{array}{r} 16 \\ 34 \\ + \ 28 \\ \hline \ \end{array}$$

46.

Tens	Ones
2	3
5	2
1	6

$$\begin{array}{r} 23 \\ 52 \\ + \ 16 \\ \hline \ \end{array}$$

36. Using Place Value to Add (No Regrouping)

☐ Add the ones.

1.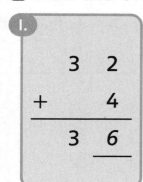

```
    3   2
+       4
─────────
    3   6
```

2.
```
    7   3
+       5
─────────
    7  ___
```

3.
```
    2   0
+       8
─────────
    2  ___
```

4.
```
    4   1
+       6
─────────
    4  ___
```

5.
```
    5   5
+       2
─────────
    5  ___
```

6.
```
    8   2
+       3
─────────
    8  ___
```

7.
```
    6   1
+       7
─────────
    6  ___
```

8.
```
    1   0
+       9
─────────
    1  ___
```

9.
```
    9   4
+       2
─────────
    9  ___
```

10.
```
    3   8
+       1
─────────
    3  ___
```

☐ Add the ones.
☐ Add the tens.

11.
```
    4   1
+   2   4
─────────
  ___ ___
```

12.
```
    3   2
+   3   1
─────────
  ___ ___
```

13.
```
    5   1
+   2   8
─────────
  ___ ___
```

14.
```
    4   4
+   4   0
─────────
  ___ ___
```

15.
```
    2   7
+   1   2
─────────
  ___ ___
```

16.
```
    6   1
+   1   8
─────────
  ___ ___
```

17.
```
    7   0
+   2   4
─────────
  ___ ___
```

18.
```
    8   9
+   1   0
─────────
  ___ ___
```

19.
```
    5   6
+   4   3
─────────
  ___ ___
```

20.
```
    7   3
+   1   5
─────────
  ___ ___
```

37. Using Place Value to Add (Regrouping)

◯ Group 10 ones.
◯ In the ▨ box, write 1 to show the group of 10 ones.
◯ In the ☐ box, write the number of ones left.

1.

$$\begin{array}{r} 9 \\ +\ 6 \\ \hline \end{array}$$

| 1 | 5 |

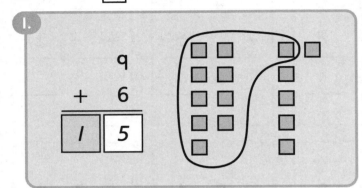

2.

$$\begin{array}{r} 8 \\ +\ 3 \\ \hline \end{array}$$

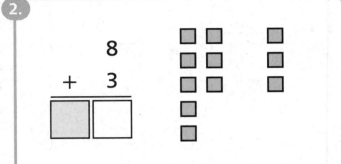

3.

$$\begin{array}{r} 5 \\ +\ 6 \\ \hline \end{array}$$

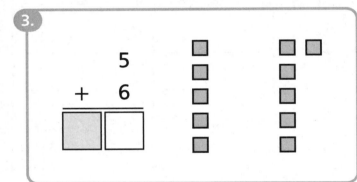

4.

$$\begin{array}{r} 7 \\ +\ 5 \\ \hline \end{array}$$

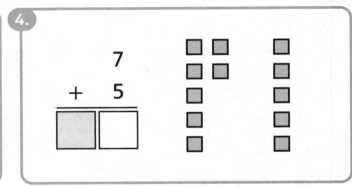

5.

$$\begin{array}{r} 8 \\ +\ 6 \\ \hline \end{array}$$

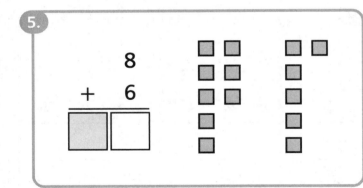

6.

$$\begin{array}{r} 7 \\ +\ 9 \\ \hline \end{array}$$

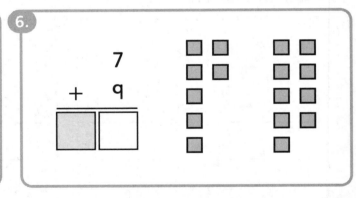

7.

$$\begin{array}{r} 5 \\ +\ 8 \\ \hline \end{array}$$

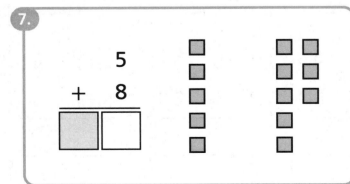

8.

$$\begin{array}{r} 9 \\ +\ 9 \\ \hline \end{array}$$

☐ Group 10 ones.
☐ Above the addition, write the number of tens.
☐ Below the addition, write the number of ones.

9.

18 + 25

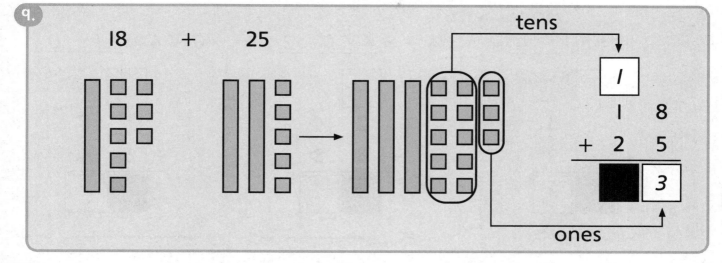

tens

	1
	1 8
+	2 5

3

ones

10.

39 + 13

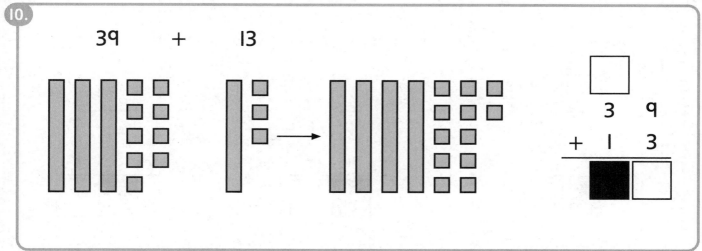

	3 9
+	1 3

11.

47 + 16

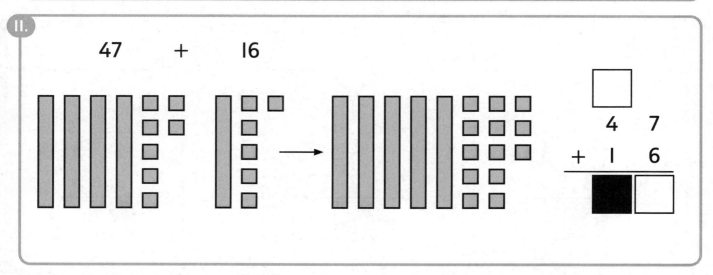

	4 7
+	1 6

◯ Add the ones using the blanks at the top.
◯ Above the tens, write 1 to show 10 ones.
◯ Below the ones, write the number of ones left.

12.

5 + 9 = __1__ __4__

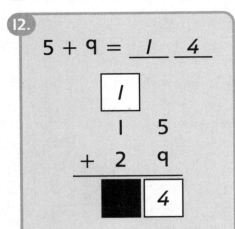

13.

4 + 8 = __1__ __2__

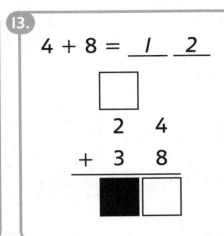

14.

6 + 4 = __1__ __0__

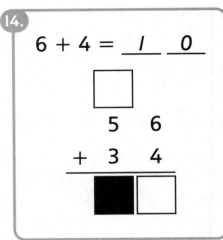

15.

7 + 5 = ___ ___

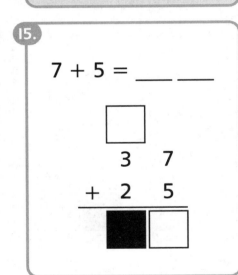

16.

6 + 9 = ___ ___

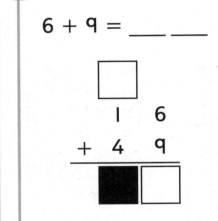

17.

___ + ___ = ___ ___

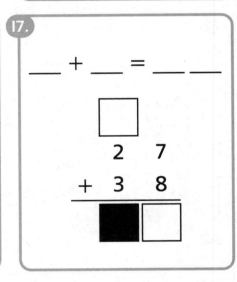

18.

___ + ___ = ___ ___

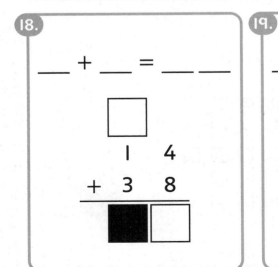

19.

___ + ___ = ___ ___

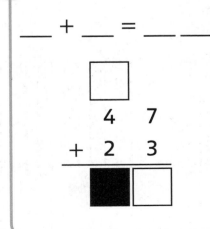

20.

___ + ___ = ___ ___

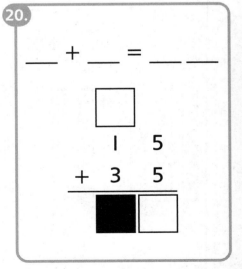

☐ Add the ones first.
☐ Then add the tens to find the total.

21.
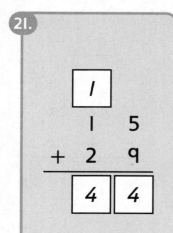
```
  [1]
    1   5
+   2   9
  ─────────
  [4] [4]
```

22.
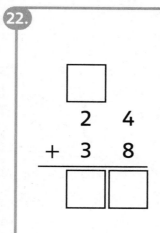
```
  [ ]
    2   4
+   3   8
  ─────────
  [ ] [ ]
```

23.
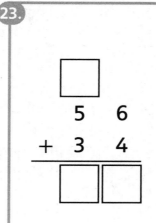
```
  [ ]
    5   6
+   3   4
  ─────────
  [ ] [ ]
```

24.
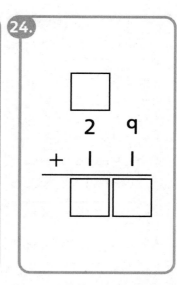
```
  [ ]
    2   9
+   1   1
  ─────────
  [ ] [ ]
```

25.
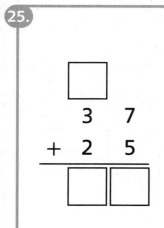
```
  [ ]
    3   7
+   2   5
  ─────────
  [ ] [ ]
```

26.
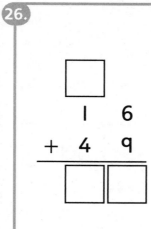
```
  [ ]
    1   6
+   4   9
  ─────────
  [ ] [ ]
```

27.
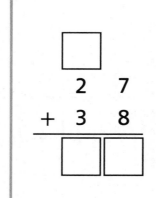
```
  [ ]
    2   7
+   3   8
  ─────────
  [ ] [ ]
```

28.
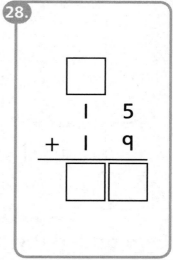
```
  [ ]
    1   5
+   1   9
  ─────────
  [ ] [ ]
```

29.
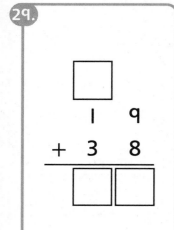
```
  [ ]
    1   9
+   3   8
  ─────────
  [ ] [ ]
```

30.
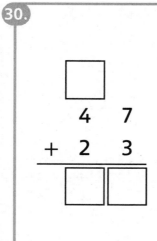
```
  [ ]
    4   7
+   2   3
  ─────────
  [ ] [ ]
```

31.
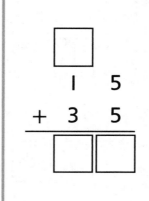
```
  [ ]
    1   5
+   3   5
  ─────────
  [ ] [ ]
```

32.
```
  [ ]
    2   8
+   3   8
  ─────────
  [ ] [ ]
```

☐ Regroup only when you need to.
☐ Add.

33.
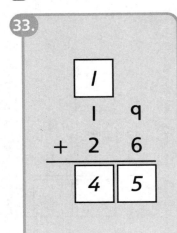
```
    1
    1  9
+   2  6
─────────
    4  5
```

34.
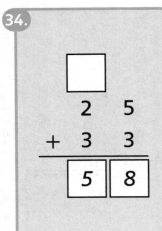
```
    2  5
+   3  3
─────────
    5  8
```

35.
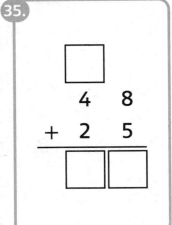
```
    4  8
+   2  5
─────────
```

36.
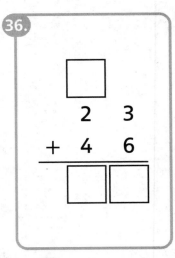
```
    2  3
+   4  6
─────────
```

37.
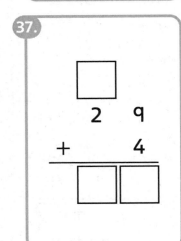
```
    2  9
+      4
─────────
```

38.
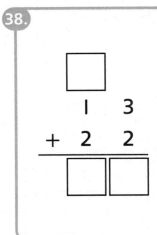
```
    1  3
+   2  2
─────────
```

39.
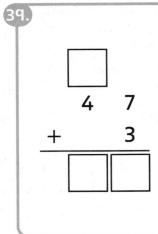
```
    4  7
+      3
─────────
```

40.
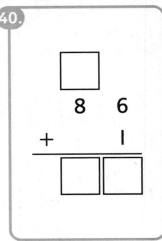
```
    8  6
+      1
─────────
```

Ivan added the tens before the ones.
☐ Circle the answers that are incorrect.

41.
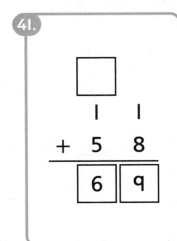
```
    1  1
+   5  8
─────────
    6  9
```

42.
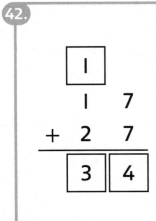
```
    1
    1  7
+   2  7
─────────
    3  4
```

43.
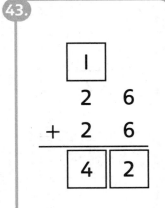
```
    1
    2  6
+   2  6
─────────
    4  2
```

44.
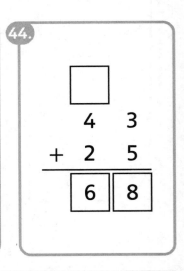
```
    4  3
+   2  5
─────────
    6  8
```

38. Addition Word Problems

☐ Add.

1.
11 more than 24

```
    2  4
+   1  1
   ┌─┬─┐
   │3│5│
   └─┴─┘
```

2.
45 more than 32

```
    3  2
+   4  5
   ┌─┬─┐
   │ │ │
   └─┴─┘
```

3.
76 more than 13

```
    1  3
+   7  6
   ┌─┬─┐
   │ │ │
   └─┴─┘
```

4.
17 more than 15

```
   ┌─┐
   │1│
   └─┘
    1  5
+   1  7
   ┌─┬─┐
   │3│2│
   └─┴─┘
```

5.
29 more than 36

```
   ┌─┐
   │ │
   └─┘
    3  6
+   2  9
   ┌─┬─┐
   │ │ │
   └─┴─┘
```

6.
48 more than 47

```
   ┌─┐
   │ │
   └─┘
    4  7
+   4  8
   ┌─┬─┐
   │ │ │
   └─┴─┘
```

7.
18 cats

25 more dogs
than cats

```
   ┌─┐
   │1│
   └─┘
    1  8
+   2  5
   ┌─┬─┐
   │4│3│ dogs
   └─┴─┘
```

8.
23 boxes

29 more bags
than boxes

```
   ┌─┐
   │ │
   └─┘
    2  3
+   2  9
   ┌─┬─┐
   │ │ │ bags
   └─┴─┘
```

9.
47 pencils

36 more pens
than pencils

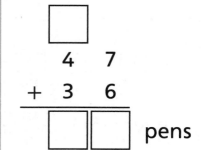

```
   ┌─┐
   │ │
   └─┘
    4  7
+   3  6
   ┌─┬─┐
   │ │ │ pens
   └─┴─┘
```

◯ Draw blocks to add.

10.

15 students were on the bus.

27 more students got on.

How many students were
on the bus altogether?

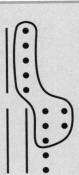

```
      1
    1   5
  + 2   7
  _____
    4 | 2
```

11.

Beth made 18 muffins on
Saturday and 24 more on Sunday.

How many did she make altogether?

```
    ☐
    1   8
  + 2   4
  _____
   ☐ ☐
```

12.

29 girls and 33 boys were at the park.

How many children were at the park?

```
    ☐
    2   9
  + 3   3
  _____
   ☐ ☐
```

13.

Ross picked 35 pears in the morning
and 39 more in the afternoon.

How many did he pick altogether?

```
    ☐
    3   5
  + 3   9
  _____
   ☐ ☐
```

◯ Draw blocks to add.

14.

Tina drew 18 circles.

Sal drew 3 more circles than Tina.

How many circles did Sal draw?

$$
\begin{array}{r}
\overset{1}{} \\
1\ 8 \\
+\ 3 \\
\hline
2\ 1
\end{array}
$$

15.

Raj pitched the ball 25 times.

Josh pitched the ball 17 more times than Raj.

How many times did Josh pitch the ball?

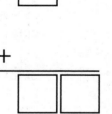

16.

Rick collected 46 rocks.

May collected 48 more rocks than Rick.

How many rocks did May collect?

17.

Hanna wrote 52 words.

Grace wrote 39 more words than Hanna.

How many words did Grace write?

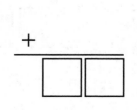

39. Subtracting a Multiple of 10

☐ Subtract 10 by taking away a tens block.

1.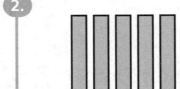

30 − 10 = __20__

2.

50 − 10 = _____

3.

80 − 10 = _____

☐ Subtract by taking away tens blocks.

4.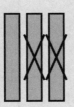

30 − 20 = __10__

5.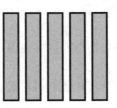

50 − 20 = _____

6.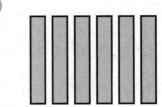

60 − 30 = _____

7.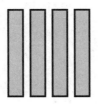

40 − 20 = _____

8.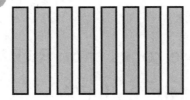

80 − 30 = _____

9.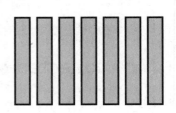

70 − 50 = _____

10.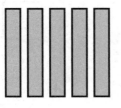

50 − 30 = _____

11.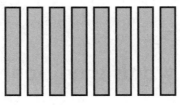

80 − 40 = _____

12.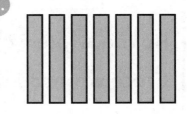

70 − 40 = _____

Subtract 10 by taking away a tens block.

13.

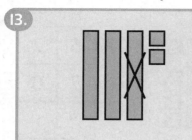

$32 - 10 = \underline{\ 22\ }$

14.

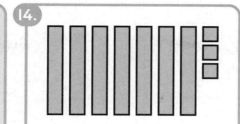

$73 - 10 = \underline{\hspace{1cm}}$

15.

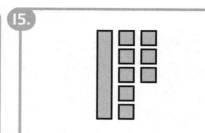

$18 - 10 = \underline{\hspace{1cm}}$

Subtract by taking away tens blocks.

16.

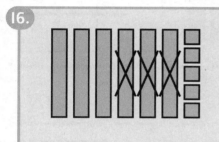

$65 - 30 = \underline{\ 35\ }$

17.

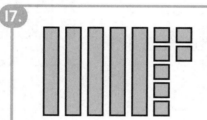

$57 - 20 = \underline{\hspace{1cm}}$

18.

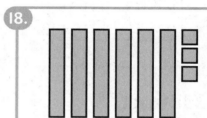

$63 - 40 = \underline{\hspace{1cm}}$

19.

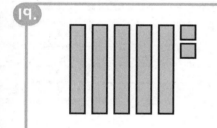

$52 - 30 = \underline{\hspace{1cm}}$

20.

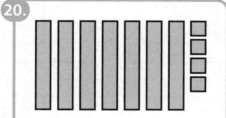

$74 - 60 = \underline{\hspace{1cm}}$

21.

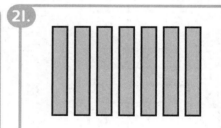

$70 - 50 = \underline{\hspace{1cm}}$

22.

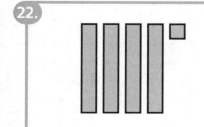

$41 - 40 = \underline{\hspace{1cm}}$

23.

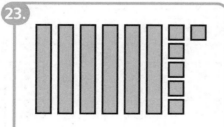

$66 - 50 = \underline{\hspace{1cm}}$

24.

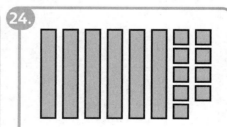

$69 - 40 = \underline{\hspace{1cm}}$

◯ Subtract by taking away tens blocks.

25.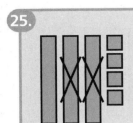

	3	4
−	2	0
	1	4

26.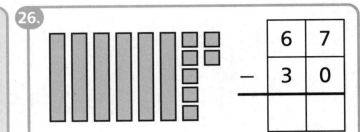

	6	7
−	3	0

27.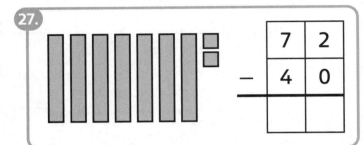

	7	2
−	4	0

28.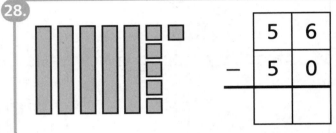

	5	6
−	5	0

◯ Subtract.

29.

	8	3
−	1	0
	7	3

30.

	7	7
−	1	0

31.

	9	2
−	1	0

32.

	3	8
−	2	0

33.

	4	8
−	2	0

34.

	8	6
−	3	0

35.

	9	7
−	4	0

36.

	8	2
−	4	0

37.

	6	1
−	5	0

38.

	9	5
−	8	0

39.

	5	4
−	4	0

40.

	9	9
−	9	0

JUMP Math Accumula

40. Using Place Value to Subtract (No Regrouping)

☐ Draw a picture to show the subtraction.
☐ Subtract.

1.
```
   46
 − 12
 ─────
   34
```
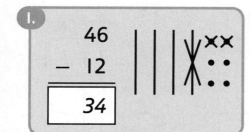

2.
```
   54
 − 31
 ─────
```
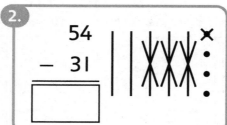

3.
```
   35
 − 13
 ─────
```

4.
```
   56
 − 24
 ─────
```

5.
```
   66
 −  4
 ─────
```

6.
```
   49
 − 30
 ─────
```

7.
```
   87
 − 46
 ─────
```

8.
```
   95
 − 61
 ─────
```

☐ Subtract.

9.

8	5
− 4	2
4	3

  8 tens 5 ones
− 4 tens 2 ones
──────────────
  4 tens 3 ones

10.

6	7
− 2	5

  6 tens 7 ones
− 2 tens 5 ones
──────────────
___ tens ___ ones

11.

9	7
− 2	1

  9 tens 7 ones
− 2 tens 1 one
──────────────
___ tens ___ ones

12.

7	3
− 4	2

  7 tens 3 ones
− 4 tens 2 ones
──────────────
___ tens ___ one

⬜ Subtract.
⬜ Check your answer by adding.

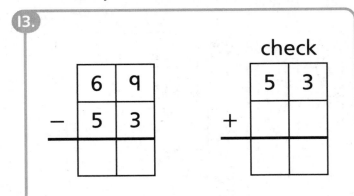

13.

	6	9
−	5	3

check

	5	3
+		

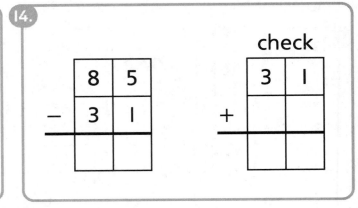

14.

	8	5
−	3	1

check

	3	1
+		

15.

	7	8
−	3	7

check

+		

16.

	6	9
−	2	4

check

+		

⬜ Subtract the ones.
⬜ Keep the tens the same.

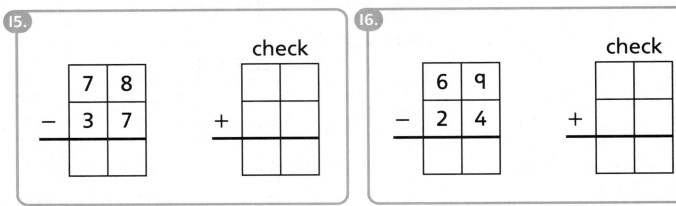

17.

	3	8
−		2
	3	*6*

18.

	7	9
−		5

19.

	2	9
−		7

20.

	5	5
−		2

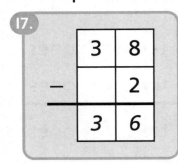 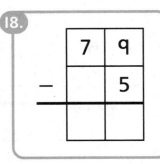 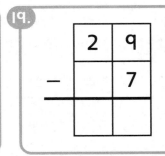

21.

	8	6
−		3

22.

	6	7
−		1

23.

	1	6
−		4

24.

	3	8
−		8

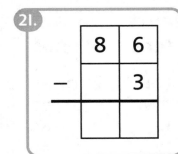 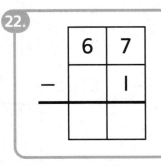

⬭ Subtract the ones. Then subtract the tens.

25.

4	5
− 2	1
2	4

26.

3	4
− 1	2

27.

5	8
− 2	3

28.

4	4
− 3	0

29.

6	9
− 1	8

30.

7	8
− 3	5

31.

8	9
− 1	9

32.

5	6
− 4	3

33.

6	1
− 5	0

34.

7	9
− 4	4

35.

8	7
− 4	3

36.

3	3
− 2	1

37.

9	7
− 5	4

38.

8	5
− 3	2

39.

9	4
− 2	1

40.

6	5
− 4	3

41. BONUS

8	7
−	
6	1

42. BONUS

9	5
−	
4	4

43. BONUS

6	9
−	
2	3

44. BONUS

9	8
−	
3	2

41. Regrouping for Subtraction

◯ What number does the picture show?

1.

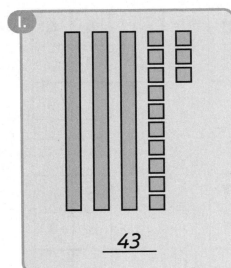

43

2.

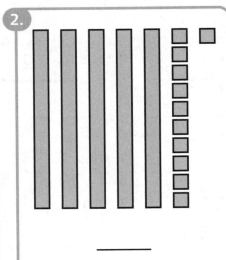

_____

3.

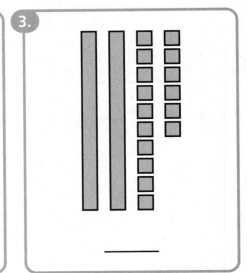

_____

◯ Take apart a ten.

4.

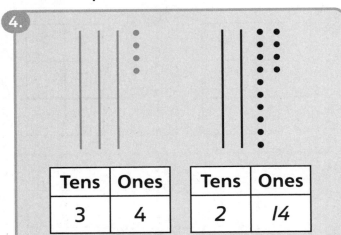

Tens	Ones
3	4

Tens	Ones
2	14

5.

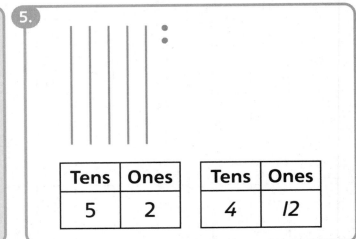

Tens	Ones
5	2

Tens	Ones
4	12

6.

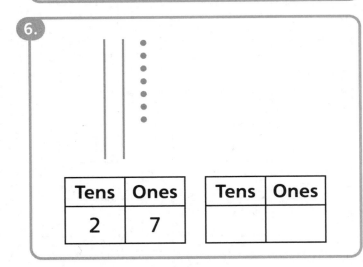

Tens	Ones
2	7

Tens	Ones

7.

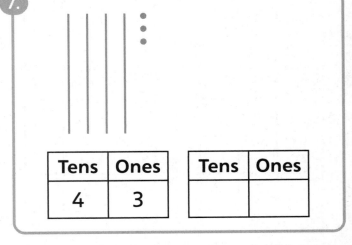

Tens	Ones
4	3

Tens	Ones

◯ Take apart a ten.
◯ Show the change in the tens and ones chart.

8.

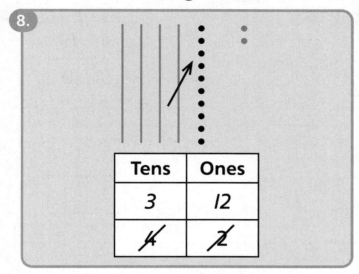

Tens	Ones
3	12
~~4~~	~~2~~

9.

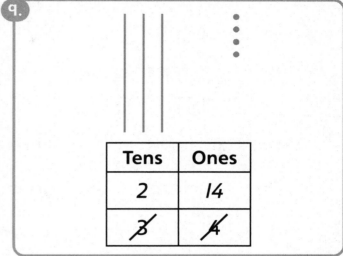

Tens	Ones
2	14
~~3~~	~~4~~

10.

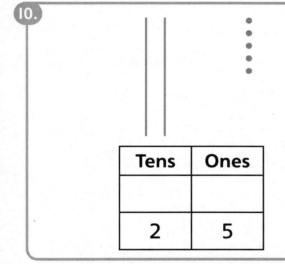

Tens	Ones
2	5

11.

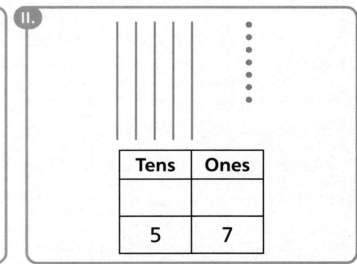

Tens	Ones
5	7

12.

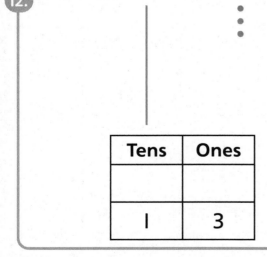

Tens	Ones
1	3

13.

Tens	Ones
3	6

◯ Take away I ten from the tens. Add 10 ones to the ones.
◯ Show the change in the tens and ones chart.

14.

50 = __5__ tens + __0__ ones

   = __4__ tens + __10__ ones

4	10
5̸	0

15.

73 = __7__ tens + __3__ ones

   = _____ tens + _____ ones

7	3

16.

85 = _____ tens + _____ ones

   = _____ tens + _____ ones

8	5

17.

5	11
6̸	1̸

18.

7	7

19.

8	6

20.

4	2

21.

3	9

22.

1	6

23.

2	3

24.

7	1

25.

4	5

26.

5	4

27.

3	0

28.

1	2

29.

6	8

30.

5	5

31.

2	9

32.

9	0

JUMP Math Accumula

42. Using Place Value to Subtract (Regrouping)

◯ Subtract.

1.

6	15
7̶	5̶
− 5	7
1	8

2.

8	3
− 5	6

3.

5	4
− 3	9

4.

4	6
− 2	7

5.

9	2
− 8	7

6.

8	1
− 5	5

7.

3	3
− 2	9

8.

4	0
− 3	6

9.

8	1
− 7	2

10.

3	6
− 2	9

11.

4	7
− 3	8

12.

6	0
− 5	7

☐ Regroup only if you need to.

☐ Subtract.

13.

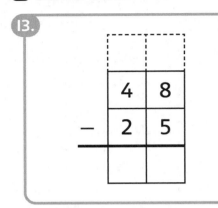

```
    4  8
-   2  5
_____
```

14.

```
    4  7
-   1  9
_____
```

15.

```
    4  9
-   1  7
_____
```

16.

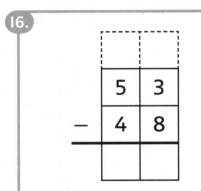

```
    5  3
-   4  8
_____
```

17.

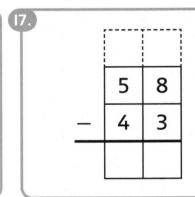

```
    5  8
-   4  3
_____
```

18.

```
    6  7
-   3  3
_____
```

19.

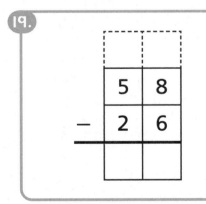

```
    5  8
-   2  6
_____
```

20.

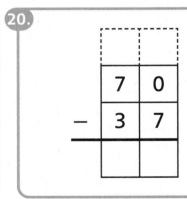

```
    7  0
-   3  7
_____
```

21.

```
    8  1
-   6  1
_____
```

22.

```
    9  8
-   2  7
_____
```

23.

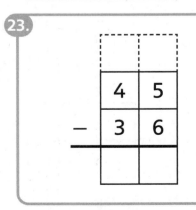

```
    4  5
-   3  6
_____
```

24.

```
    9  0
-   4  8
_____
```

JUMP Math Accumula

☐ Regroup only if you need to.
☐ Subtract.

25.

5	13
~~6~~	~~3~~
− 3	5
2	8

26.

7	3
− 2	9

27.

5	1
− 3	3

28.

8	4
− 6	7

29.

3	8
− 1	7

30.

4	5
− 2	6

31.

8	8
− 1	4

32.

2	6
− 1	9

33.

9	7
− 1	3

34.

7	3
− 2	9

35.

2	2
− 1	4

36.

8	6
− 6	1

37.

Rita did this subtraction.

What mistake did she make?

1	5
6	~~5~~
− 3	8
3	7

43. Subtraction Word Problems

☐ Draw blocks to subtract.

1.

There were 27 raisins in a box.

Abdul ate 13 raisins.

How many raisins are left?

	2	7
−	1	3
	1	4

2.

93 bees were in a hive.

44 bees flew away.

How many bees stayed in the hive?

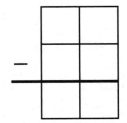

3.

86 ants marched in a line.

Some ants wandered off.

52 kept marching.

How many ants wandered off?

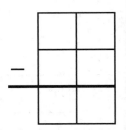

4.

Blanca had 75 pennies.

She put some in a jar. Now she has 39 pennies.

How many pennies did she put in the jar?

5. BONUS

Amy ate 25 grapes. There were 42 grapes before.

How many grapes are left?

☐ Draw blocks to subtract.

6.

Carl has 25 apples.

12 apples are red. The rest are green.

How many apples are green?

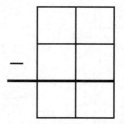

	2	5
−	1	2

7.

57 guppies are in a fish tank.

29 are black. The rest are blue.

How many are blue?

−		

8.

Jen has 21 baseball cards.

Mike has 9 baseball cards.

How many more baseball cards does Jen have?

−		

9.

Anwar has 23 stickers.

Vicki has 17 stickers.

How many more stickers does Anwar have?

10. BONUS

There are 24 blue pencils and 49 red pencils in a box.

How many more red pencils are there?

44. Measuring Length

Units must be the same length. There must be no spaces between units.

◻ Is the measurement correct? Write ✓ or ✗.

1.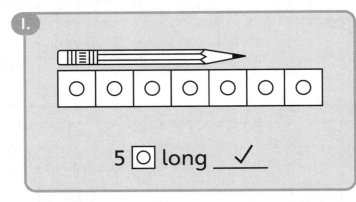

5 ▣ long ___✓___

2.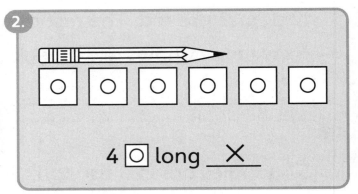

4 ▣ long ___✗___

3.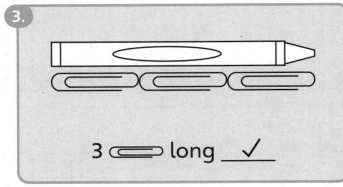

3 ⬭ long ___✓___

4.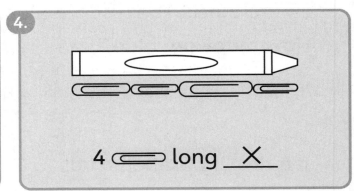

4 ⬭ long ___✗___

5.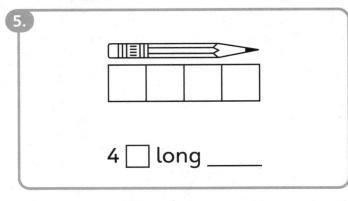

4 ◻ long _____

6.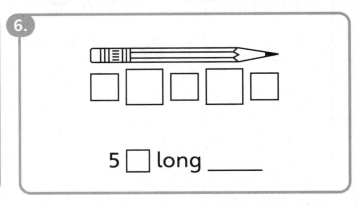

5 ◻ long _____

7.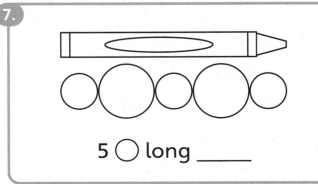

5 ◯ long _____

8.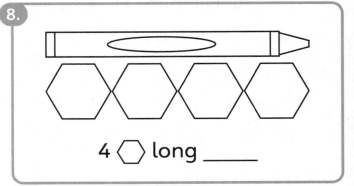

4 ⬡ long _____

○ Is the measurement correct? Write ✓ or ✗.

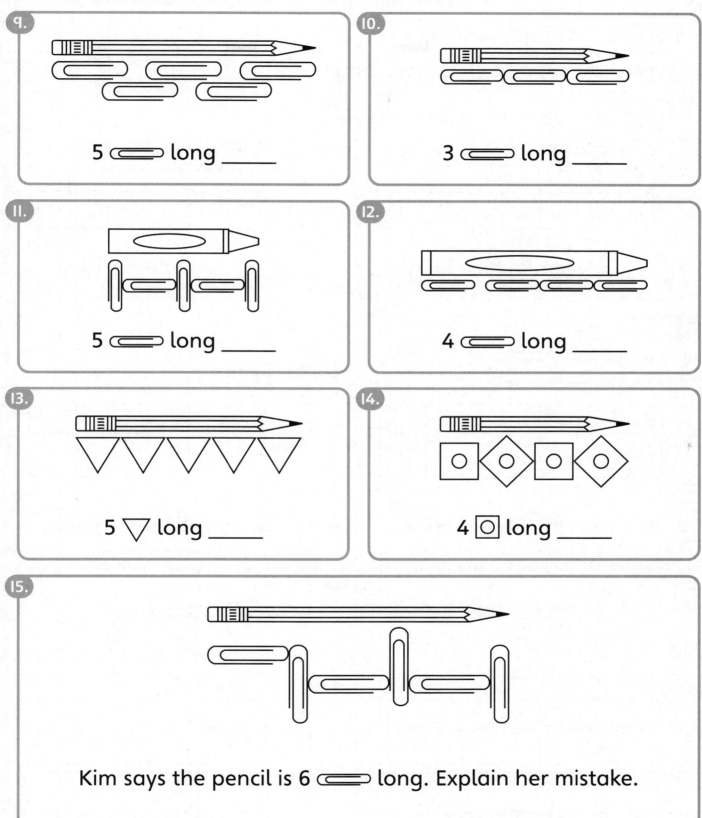

9.

5 ⬭ long _____

10.

3 ⬭ long _____

11.

5 ⬭ long _____

12.

4 ⬭ long _____

13.

5 ▽ long _____

14.

4 ▢ long _____

15.

Kim says the pencil is 6 ⬭ long. Explain her mistake.

_____

45. Measuring in Centimeters

A  is I **centimeter** long.

☐ Write how many centimeters long.

1.

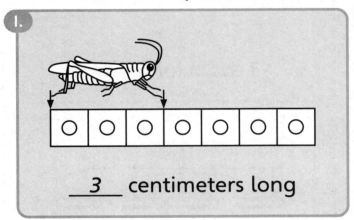

____3____ centimeters long

2.

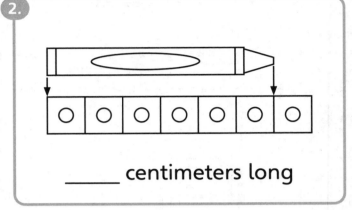

_____ centimeters long

3.

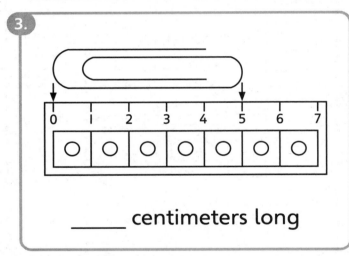

_____ centimeters long

4.

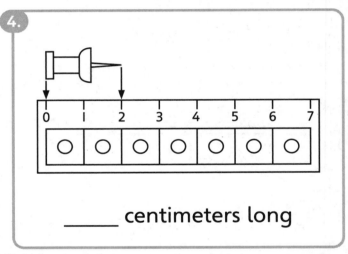

_____ centimeters long

5.

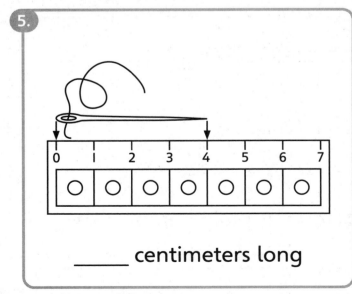

_____ centimeters long

6.

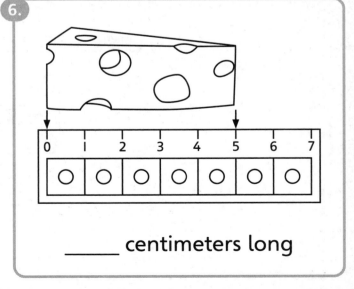

_____ centimeters long

We can write **cm** for **c**enti**m**eter.
☐ Measure how many cm.

7.

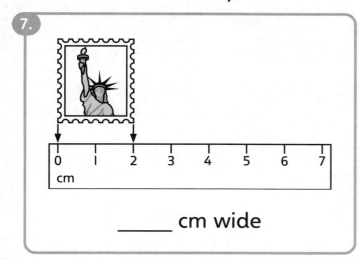

_____ cm wide

8.

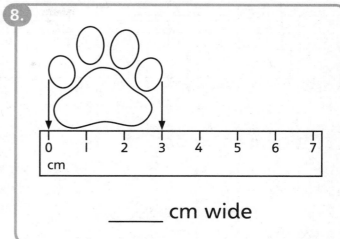

_____ cm wide

9.

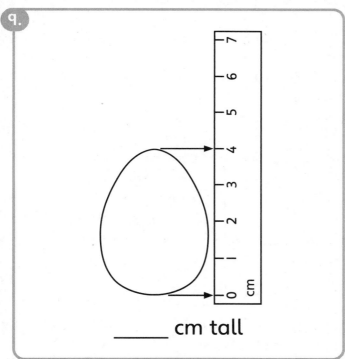

_____ cm tall

10.

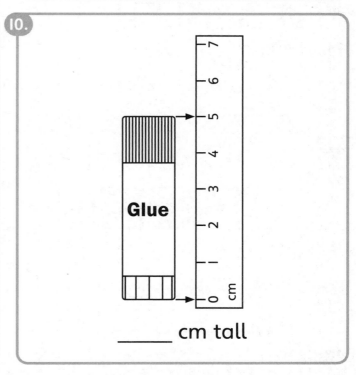

_____ cm tall

11.

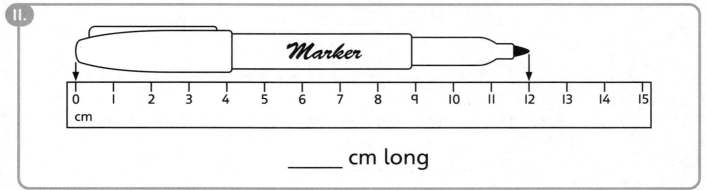

_____ cm long

☐ Measure the object.

12.

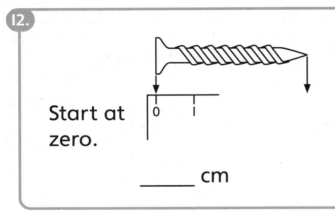

Start at zero.

_____ cm

13.

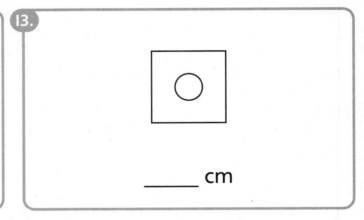

_____ cm

14.

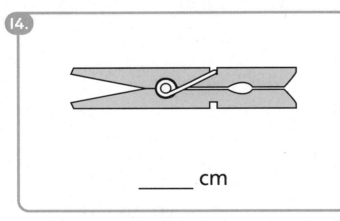

_____ cm

15.

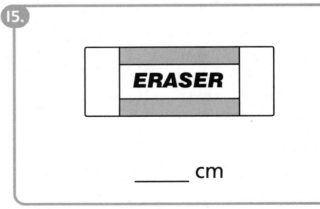

_____ cm

16.

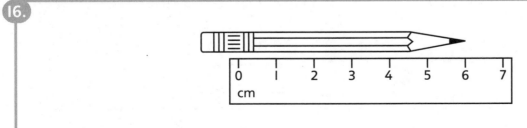

Sam says the pencil is 6 cm long. Explain his mistake.

_____

JUMP Math Accumula

46. Length and Subtraction

How far apart are the arrows?
☐ Count the jumps, starting at zero.

1.

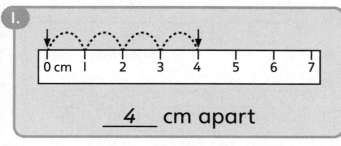

_____4_____ cm apart

2.

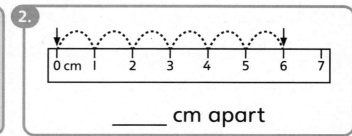

_____ cm apart

3.

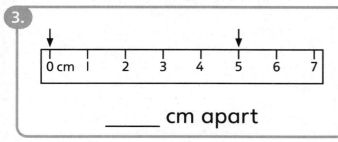

_____ cm apart

4.

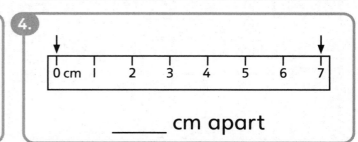

_____ cm apart

5.

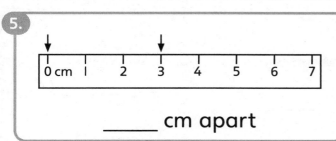

_____ cm apart

6.

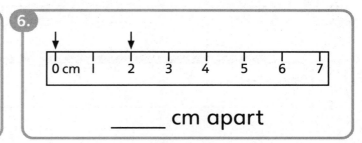

_____ cm apart

How far apart are the arrows?
☐ Count the jumps.

7.

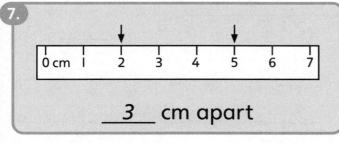

_____3_____ cm apart

8.

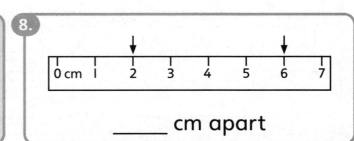

_____ cm apart

9.

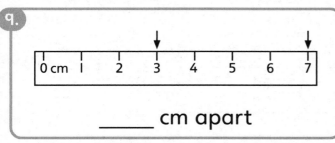

_____ cm apart

10.

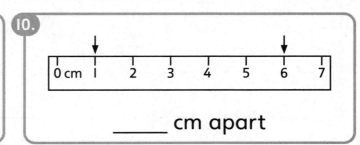

_____ cm apart

⬭ Measure the length of the line or object.

11.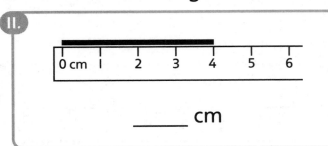

_____ cm

12.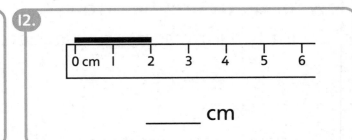

_____ cm

13.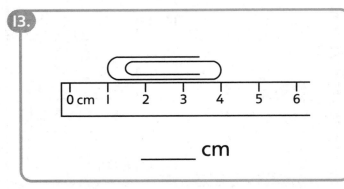

_____ cm

14.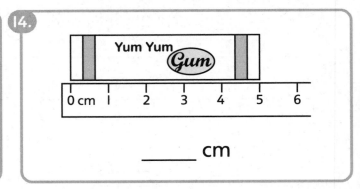

_____ cm

15.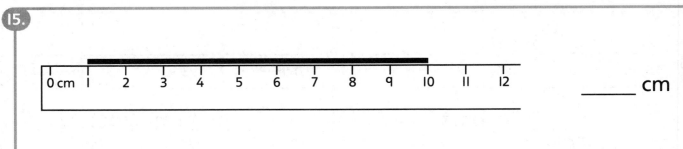

_____ cm

16.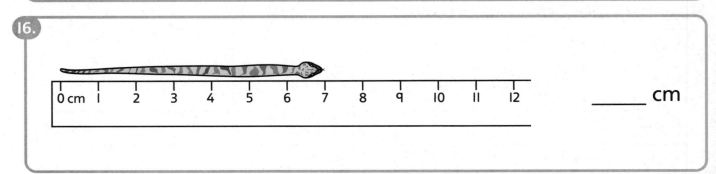

_____ cm

17.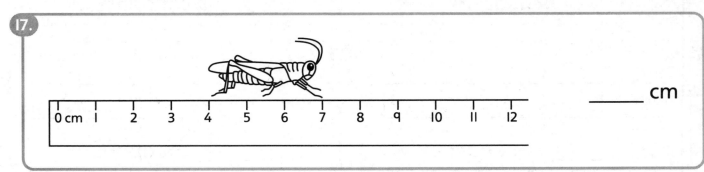

_____ cm

Bo counts jumps to find
the length.

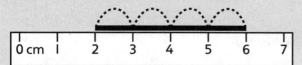

The line is __4__ cm long.

Jen subtracts to find
the length.

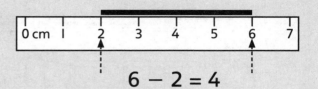

$6 - 2 = 4$

The line is __4__ cm long.

⬡ Subtract to find the length.

18.

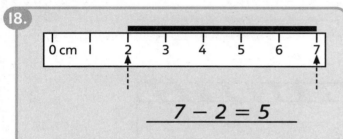

$7 - 2 = 5$

The line is __5__ cm long.

19.

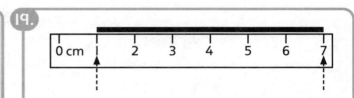

_____

The line is _____ cm long.

20.

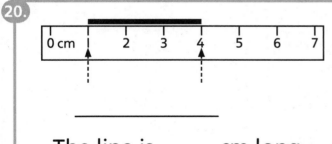

_____

The line is _____ cm long.

21.

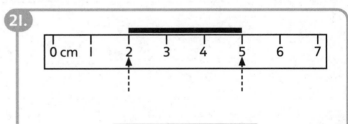

_____

The line is _____ cm long.

22.

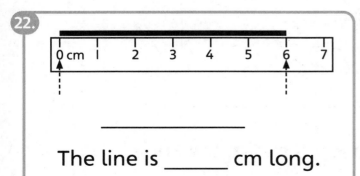

_____

The line is _____ cm long.

23.

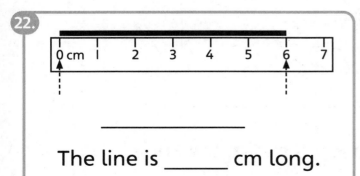

_____

The line is _____ cm long.

47. Comparing Lengths

☐ How much longer?

1.

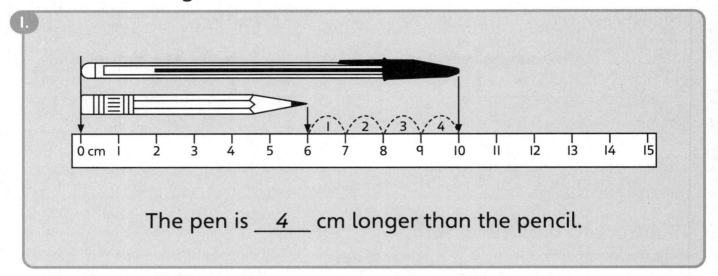

The pen is __4__ cm longer than the pencil.

2.

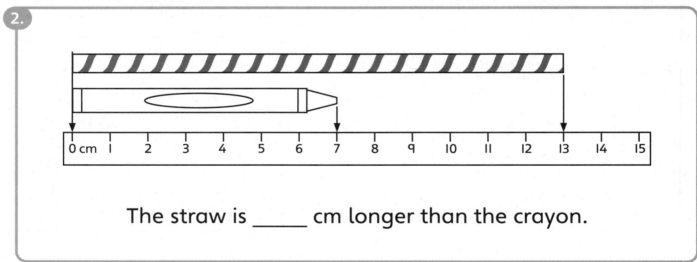

The straw is _____ cm longer than the crayon.

3.

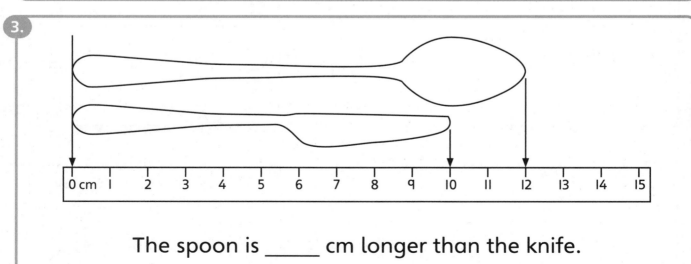

The spoon is _____ cm longer than the knife.

⬭ How much longer?

4.

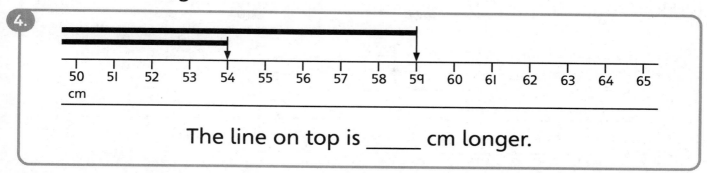

The line on top is _____ cm longer.

5.

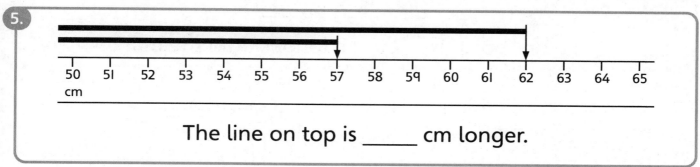

The line on top is _____ cm longer.

6.

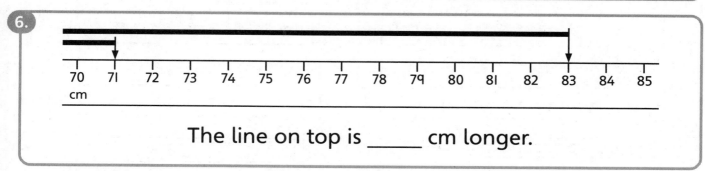

The line on top is _____ cm longer.

7.

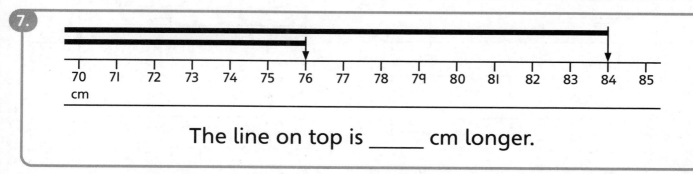

The line on top is _____ cm longer.

8.

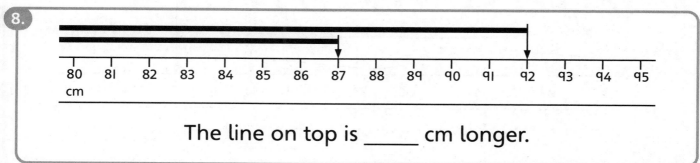

The line on top is _____ cm longer.

48. Subtraction and Length

☐ How much longer? Write a subtraction sentence.

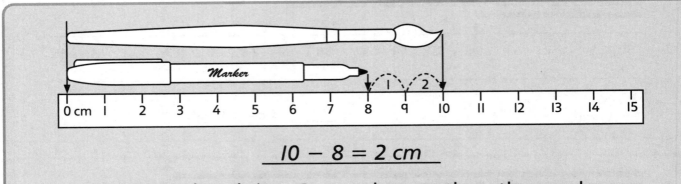

$$10 - 8 = 2 \text{ cm}$$

The paint brush is __2__ cm longer than the marker.

1.

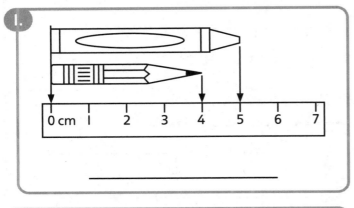

_____

2.

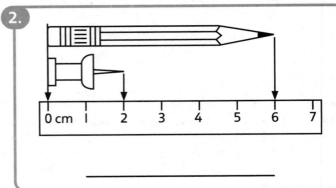

_____

3.

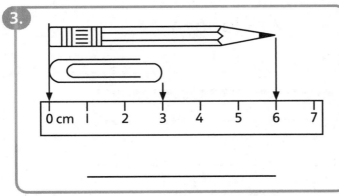

_____

4.

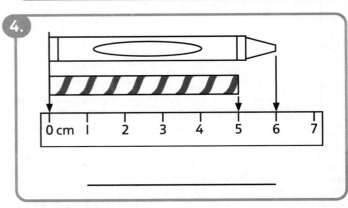

_____

5.

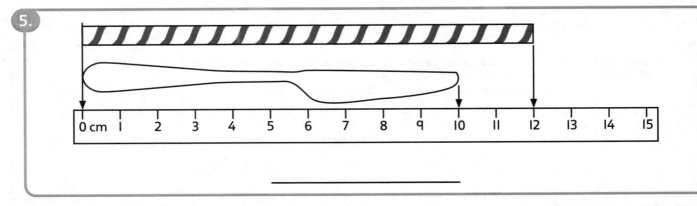

_____

JUMP Math Accumula

⬜ Measure the animals.

⬜ How much longer is the worm? Show your work.

6.

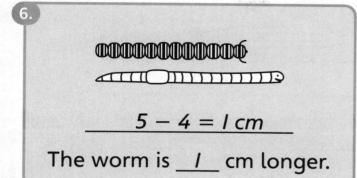

$$5 - 4 = 1\ cm$$

The worm is __1__ cm longer.

7.

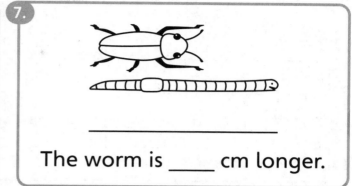

_____

The worm is ____ cm longer.

8.

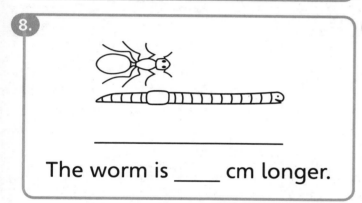

_____

The worm is ____ cm longer.

9.

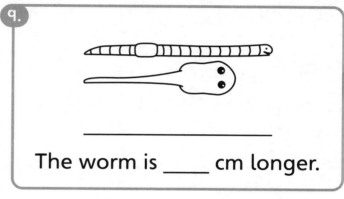

_____

The worm is ____ cm longer.

⬜ Use the measurements to answer the questions.

10.

crayon	paper clip	pen	pencil
5 cm	3 cm	8 cm	10 cm

How much longer than the pen is the pencil? _____

How much longer than the paper clip is the crayon? _____

How much shorter than the pen is the paper clip? _____

11. A turtle is 12 cm long. A fish is 5 cm long.
How much longer is the turtle?

12. A bus is 7 m long. A truck is 11 m long.
How much longer than the bus is the truck?

49. Addition and Length

How long are the paper clip and pencil together?

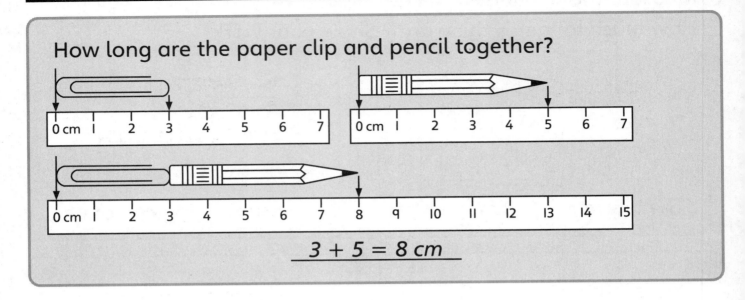

$$3 + 5 = 8 \text{ cm}$$

☐ Draw an arrow where the pencil ends.
☐ Write the addition sentence.

1.

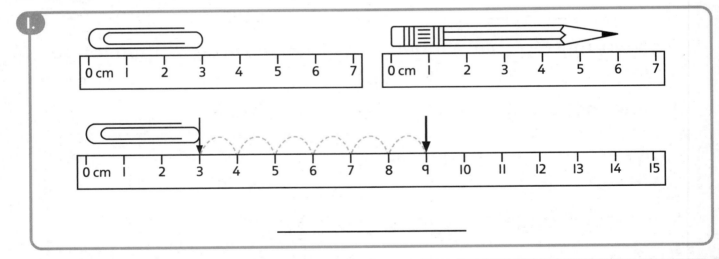

_____

2.

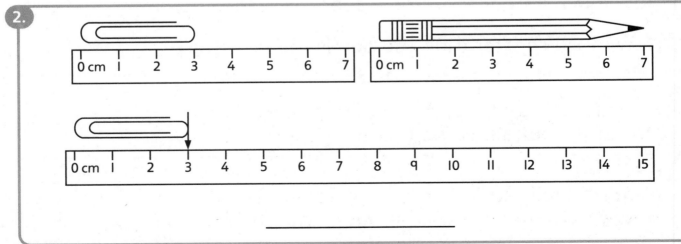

_____

The paper clip is 3 cm long. The tack is 2 cm long.

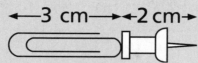

←—3 cm—→ ←2 cm→

Emma writes an addition sentence for the total length.

$3 + 2 = 5$ cm

☐ Find the total length. Write the addition sentence.

3.
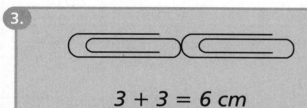

$3 + 3 = 6$ cm

4.
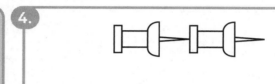

_____

5.
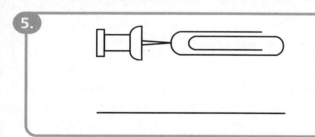

_____

6.
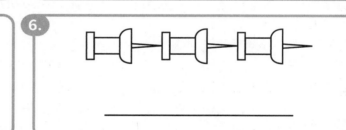

_____

☐ Find the total length. Write the addition sentence.

crayon	paper clip	pen	pencil
5 cm	3 cm	8 cm	10 cm

7.
a pen and a pencil

_____

8.
a pencil and a paper clip

_____

9.
a pen and a crayon

_____

10.
2 pencils

_____

50. Addition and Length (Advanced)

◯ Measure the parts of the string.
◯ Write an addition sentence to find the total length.

1.

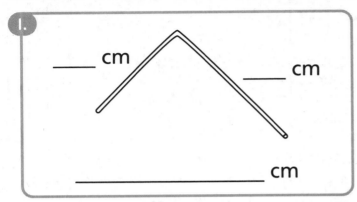

_____ cm

_____ cm

_____ cm

2.

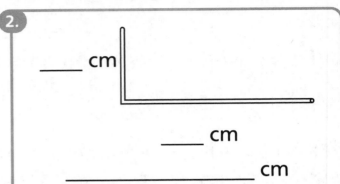

_____ cm

_____ cm

_____ cm

3.

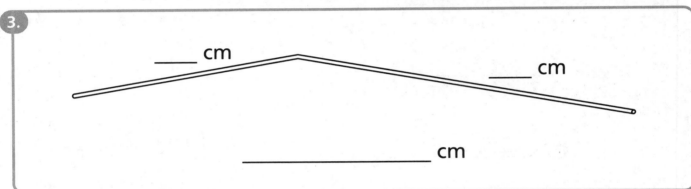

_____ cm

_____ cm

_____ cm

4.

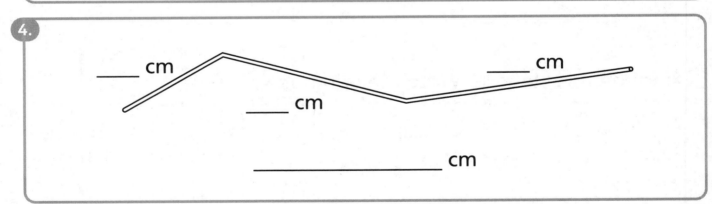

_____ cm

_____ cm

_____ cm

_____ cm

5. BONUS

A table is 2 m long.

Write an addition sentence for each length.

2 tables   3 tables   4 tables

_2 + 2 = 4 m_   _____   _____

Find the total distance the ant travels.

6.

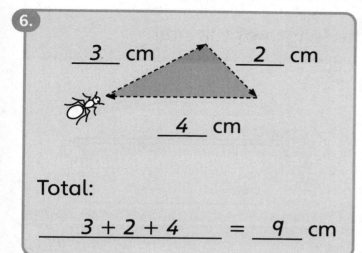

_3_ cm   _2_ cm

_4_ cm

Total:

_____3 + 2 + 4_____ = _9_ cm

7.

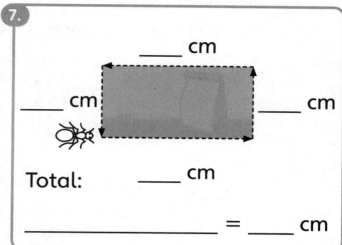

____ cm

____ cm   ____ cm

Total: ____ cm

_____ = ____ cm

8.

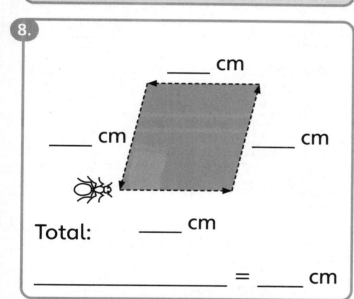

____ cm

____ cm   ____ cm

Total: ____ cm

_____ = ____ cm

9.

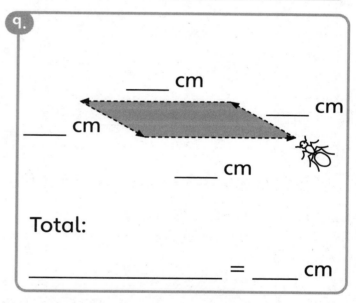

____ cm

____ cm   ____ cm

____ cm

Total:

_____ = ____ cm

10.

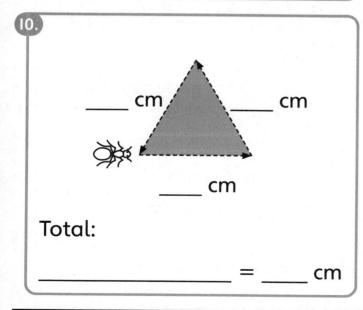

____ cm   ____ cm

____ cm

Total:

_____ = ____ cm

11.

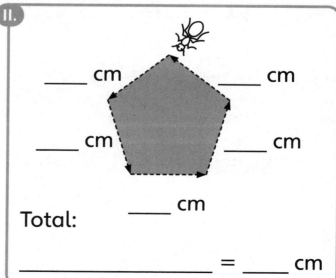

____ cm   ____ cm

____ cm   ____ cm

____ cm

Total:

_____ = ____ cm

5I. Finding Lengths from Differences

The screw is 4 cm long.

◯ Write an addition sentence for the length of the nail.

1.

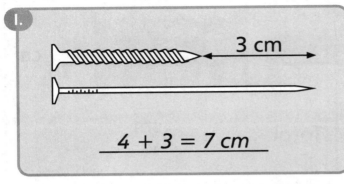

3 cm

4 + 3 = 7 cm

2.

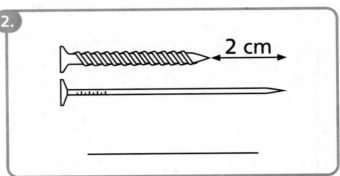

2 cm

_____

3.

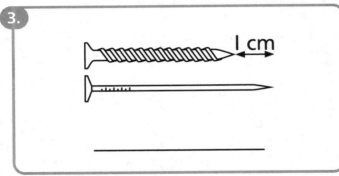

1 cm

_____

4.

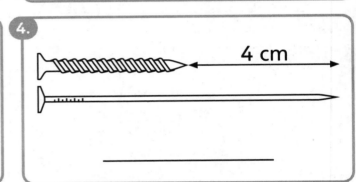

4 cm

_____

◯ The screw is 3 cm long. Find the length of the nail.

◯ Check by measuring.

5.

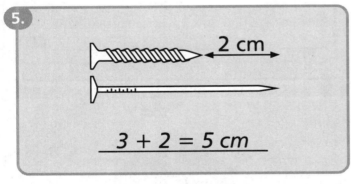

2 cm

3 + 2 = 5 cm

6.

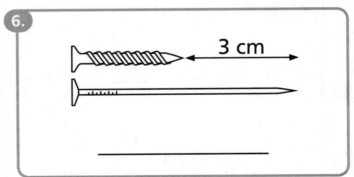

3 cm

_____

7.

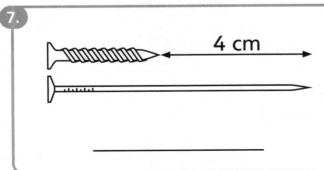

4 cm

_____

8.

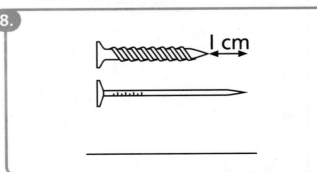

1 cm

_____

⬡ Draw the line.

9. 2 cm longer than the screw

10. 3 cm longer than the screw

11. I cm shorter than the screw

12. 2 cm shorter than the screw

The screw is 5 cm long.

⬡ Write an addition sentence to find the length of the pencil.

13.

2 cm

_____

14.

3 cm

_____

15. A comic is 20 cm wide. A book is 6 cm wider.
How wide is the book?

16. A truck is 10 m long. A car is 6 m shorter.
How long is the car?

52. Solving Problems

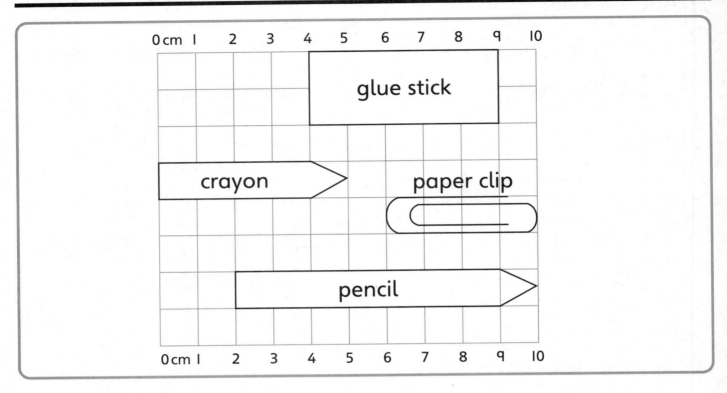

☐ How many cm long?

1.

crayon	glue stick	paper clip	pencil
_____ cm	_____ cm	_____ cm	_____ cm

☐ If you put the objects in a row, how long would they be?

2.

crayon and paper clip _____

pencil and crayon _____

glue stick and pencil _____

paper clip and glue stick _____

3. BONUS

crayon, pencil, and glue stick _____

4.

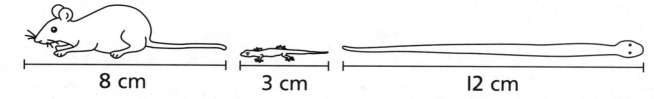

8 cm	3 cm	12 cm

How much longer than the lizard is the mouse? _____

How much longer than the mouse is the snake? _____

How much shorter than the snake is the lizard? _____

Which is the longest animal? _____

5.

Car	Length
large truck	22 m
van	6 m
small truck	10 m

How much longer than the van is the large truck? _____

How long are the van and the small truck together? _____

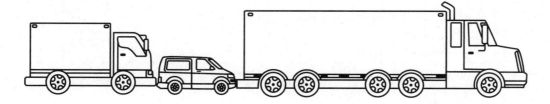

All three cars are parked in a row. How long is the row?

_____

Jen's car is 2 m shorter than the van. How long is Jen's car?

_____

53. More and Fewer

☐ Draw ◯ or △ to show which is fewer.

1.	Which is fewer?
◯ ◯ ◯ ◯ ◯ ◯ △ △ △ △	△
◯ ◯ △ △ △ △ △	
△ △ △ △ △ △ △ ◯ ◯ ◯	
△ △ △ △ ◯ ◯ ◯ ◯ ◯ ◯ ◯	

☐ Circle **more** or **fewer** △.

2.	More or fewer △?
◯ ◯ ◯ △ △ △ △ △ △	(more) fewer
◯ ◯ ◯ ◯ △ △	more fewer
△ △ △ △ △ ◯ ◯ ◯ ◯ ◯ ◯ ◯	more fewer
△ △ △ △ △ △ △ ◯ ◯ ◯ ◯ ◯ ◯	more fewer

☐ Draw ◯ or △ to show which is fewer.
☐ Write how many fewer.

3.		Which is fewer?	How many fewer?
◯ ◯ ◯ △ △ △ △ △		◯	2
◯ ◯ ◯ ◯ ◯ ◯ △ △			
△ △ △ △ ◯ ◯ ◯ ◯ ◯ ◯ ◯			
△ △ △ △ △ △ △ △ △ ◯ ◯ ◯ ◯			

☐ Draw ◯ or △ to show which is more.
☐ Find how many more.

4.	Which is more?	How many more?
5 ◯ or 8 △	△	8 − 5 = 3
12 ◯ or 7 △		___ − ___ = ___
14 ◯ or 12 △		___ − ___ = ___
9 ◯ or 12 △		___ − ___ = ___
11 ◯ or 6 △		___ − ___ = ___
10 ◯ or 15 △		___ − ___ = ___

☐ Underline who has fewer.
☐ Find how many fewer.

5.	How many fewer?
<u>Tess</u> has 5 shells. Jack has 8 shells.	_8_ – _5_ = _3_
Emma has 17 shells. Ted has 7 shells.	___ – ___ = ___
Ray has 14 shells. Grace has 18 shells.	___ – ___ = ___
Ava has 9 shells. Tony has 15 shells.	___ – ___ = ___
Nina has 11 shells. Ivan has 4 shells.	___ – ___ = ___

☐ Find how many more or fewer.

6.

Yu has 8 raisins. Bill has 12 raisins.

How many more raisins does Bill have?   ___ – ___ = ___

7.

Alex has 13 raisins. Ethan has 2 raisins.

How many fewer raisins does Ethan have?   ___ – ___ = ___

8.

Clara has 13 raisins. Abdul has 2 raisins.

How many more raisins does Clara have?   ___ – ___ = ___

54. Compare Using Pictures

☐ Circle who has more. Underline who has fewer.
☐ Draw triangles for Rosa.

1.

Ⓡⓞⓢⓐ has 3 more △ than <u>Sam</u>.

Sam	△	△	△	△	△			
Rosa	△	△	△	△	△	△	△	△

2.

Rosa has 3 fewer △ than Sam.

Sam	△	△	△	△	△			
Rosa								

3.

Rosa has 1 more △ than Sam.

Sam	△	△	△	△	△			
Rosa								

4.

Rosa has 2 more △ than Sam.

Sam	△	△	△	△	△			
Rosa								

5.

Rosa has 4 fewer △ than Sam.

Sam	△	△	△	△	△			
Rosa								

☐ Draw triangles for Beth.
☐ Circle how many triangles Beth has.

6.

Greg has 5 △. △ △ △ △ △   (5 + 2)

Beth has 2 more △ than Greg. △ △ △ △ △ △ △   5 − 2

7.

Greg has 3 △. △ △ △   3 + 2

Beth has 2 fewer △ than Greg.   3 − 2

8.

Greg has 6 △. △ △ △ △ △ △   6 + 3

Beth has 3 more △ than Greg.   6 − 3

9.

Greg has 4 △. △ △ △ △   4 + 3

Beth has 3 fewer △ than Greg.   4 − 3

10.

Greg has 7 △. △ △ △ △ △ △ △   7 + 1

Beth has 1 fewer △ than Greg.   7 − 1

JUMP Math Accumula

55. Comparing and Word Problems (I)

◯ Circle which is more. Underline which is fewer.
◯ Find how many circles.

I.	△		How many ◯?
5	There are 3 more ◯ than △.		_5 + 3_ = _8_
6	There are 3 fewer ◯ than △.		_6 –_ = ___
4	There are 2 more ◯ than △.		___ = ___
9	There are 6 fewer ◯ than △.		___ = ___
15	There are 4 fewer ◯ than △.		___ = ___
13	There are 5 fewer ◯ than △.		___ = ___
9	There are 4 more ◯ than △.		___ = ___
21	There are 5 more ◯ than △.		___ = ___
27	There are 3 fewer ◯ than △.		___ = ___
39	There are 6 fewer ◯ than △.		___ = ___

○ Circle which is more. Underline which is fewer.
○ Add or subtract.

2.

Mona has 25 apples.

She has 12 more (pears) than apples.

How many pears does Mona have?

	2	5
+	1	2

3.

Mark has 46 red flowers.

He has 17 fewer yellow flowers than (red) flowers.

How many yellow flowers does Mark have?

4.

Tim has 93 blocks.

He has 46 fewer balls than blocks.

How many balls does Tim have?

5.

Lynn drew 28 circles.

She drew 17 more triangles than circles.

How many triangles did Lynn draw?

56. Comparing and Word Problems (2)

☐ Underline **more** or **fewer**.

1. Maria has 3 more stickers than Bob.
Bob has more / <u>fewer</u> stickers than Maria.

Maria has 3 fewer stickers than Bob.
Bob has more / fewer stickers than Maria.

2. Carlos has 2 more stickers than Jen.
Jen has more / fewer stickers than Carlos.

Carlos has 2 fewer stickers than Jen.
Jen has more / fewer stickers than Carlos.

☐ Circle who has more. Underline who has fewer.
☐ Draw triangles for Rani.

3. (Kyle) has 2 more △ than <u>Rani</u>.

Kyle	△	△	△	△	△			
Rani	△	△	△					

4. Kyle has 2 fewer △ than Rani.

Kyle	△	△	△	△	△			
Rani								

5. Kyle has 3 more △ than Rani.

Kyle	△	△	△	△	△			
Rani								

Liz has 10 grapes.
◯ Circle who has more grapes. Underline who has fewer grapes.
◯ Fill in the table.

6.	Does Jon have more or fewer?	How many does Jon have?
(Liz) has 2 more grapes than <u>Jon</u>.	fewer	10 (−) 2
Liz has 2 fewer grapes than Jon.		10 ◯ 2
Liz has 3 more grapes than Jon.		10 ◯ 3
Liz has 3 fewer grapes than Jon.		10 ◯ 3

◯ Circle who has more. Underline who has fewer.
◯ Fill in the table.

7.	Does Sal have more or fewer?	How many does Sal have?
Amy has 8 grapes. <u>Amy</u> has 3 fewer grapes than (Sal.)	more	8 + 3 = 11
Amy has 8 grapes. Amy has 3 more grapes than Sal.		_____ = ___
Amy has 6 grapes. Amy has 5 fewer grapes than Sal.		_____ = ___
Amy has 11 grapes. Amy has 7 more grapes than Sal.		_____ = ___

○ Circle who has more pencils. Underline who has fewer pencils.
○ Find how many pencils David has.

8.

Hanna has 26 pencils.

<u>Hanna</u> has 13 fewer pencils than (David.)

How many pencils does David have?

$$\begin{array}{r} 2\ 6 \\ +\ 1\ 3 \\ \hline \end{array}$$

9.

Hanna has 43 pencils.

(Hanna) has 22 more pencils than <u>David</u>.

How many pencils does David have?

10.

Hanna has 26 pencils.

Hanna has 37 fewer pencils than David.

How many pencils does David have?

11.

Hanna has 65 pencils.

Hanna has 18 more pencils than David.

How many pencils does David have?

12.

Hanna has 79 pencils.

Hanna has 43 more pencils than David.

How many pencils does David have?

57. Place Value with 3 Digits (I)

☐ Circle groups of 10 tens.
☐ Draw the same number using hundreds and tens blocks.

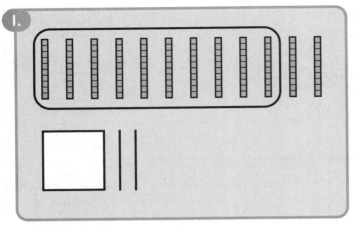

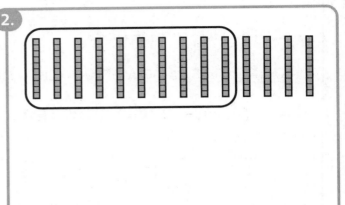

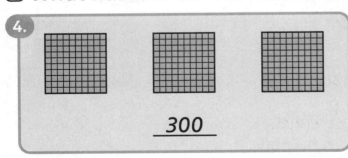

☐ What number do the hundreds blocks show?

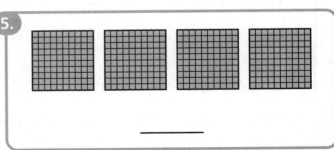

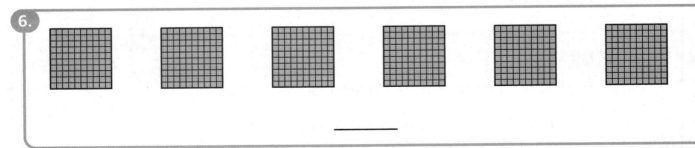

Draw hundreds blocks to show the number.

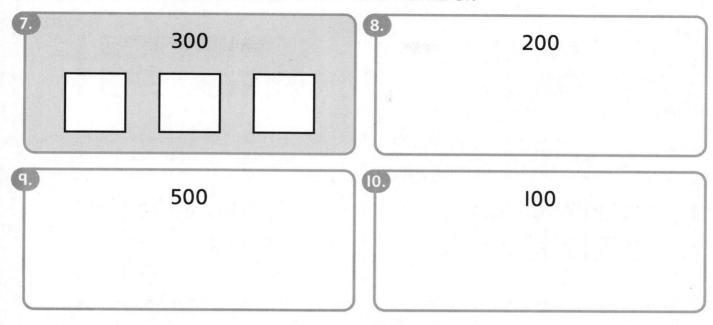

7. 300

8. 200

9. 500

10. 100

Write the number of hundreds blocks.

Write the number that the tens and ones blocks show.

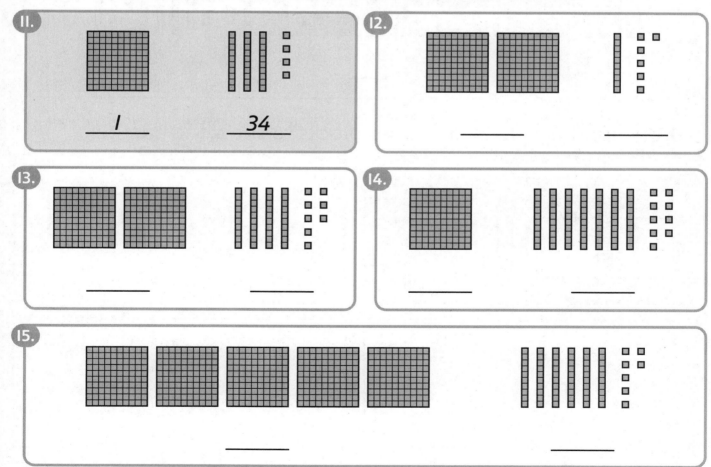

11. ___1___   ___34___

12. _____   _____

13. _____   _____

14. _____   _____

15. _____   _____

○ What number do the blocks show?

16.
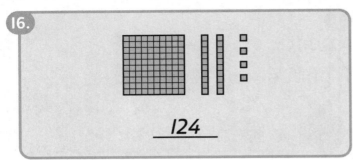
_124_

17.
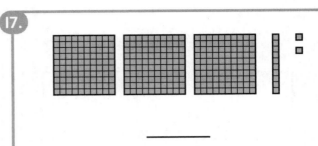
_____

18.
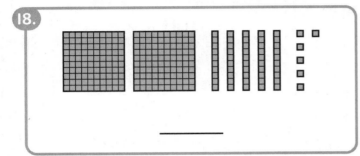
_____

19.
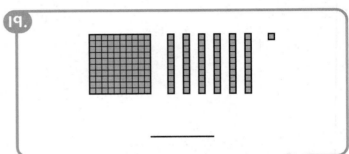
_____

20.
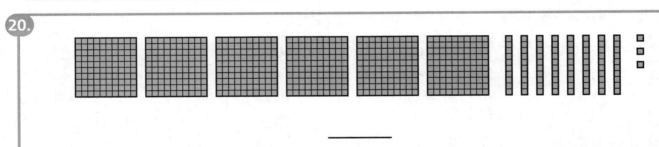
_____

○ Draw hundreds, tens, and ones blocks to show the number.

21.
235
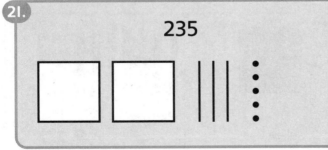

22.
142
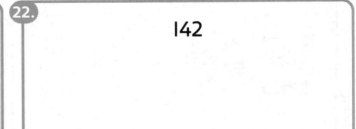

23.
264
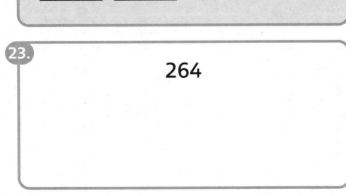

24.
321
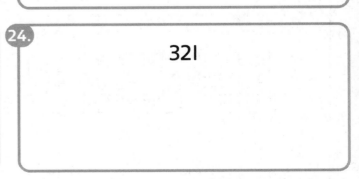

JUMP Math Accumula

58. Place Value with 3 Digits (2)

◻ Count the blocks to fill in the **base ten chart**.

1.

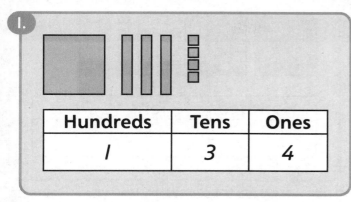

Hundreds	Tens	Ones
1	3	4

2.

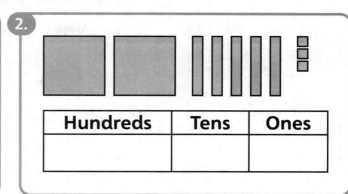

Hundreds	Tens	Ones

3.

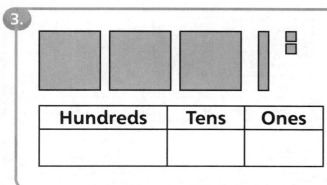

Hundreds	Tens	Ones

4.

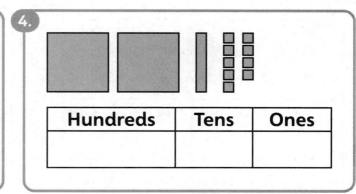

Hundreds	Tens	Ones

◻ Draw the number of blocks shown in the base ten chart.

5.

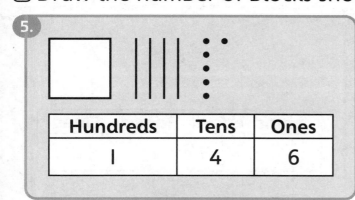

Hundreds	Tens	Ones
1	4	6

6.

Hundreds	Tens	Ones
2	5	3

7.

Hundreds	Tens	Ones
2	3	7

8.

Hundreds	Tens	Ones
1	2	4

◯ Count the blocks to fill in the base ten chart.

9.

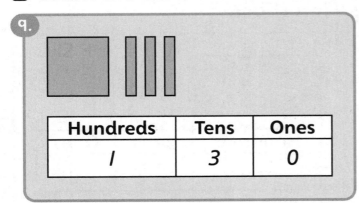

Hundreds	Tens	Ones
1	3	0

10.

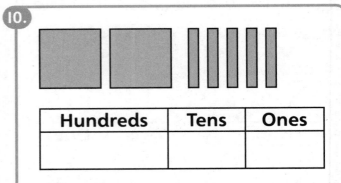

Hundreds	Tens	Ones

11.

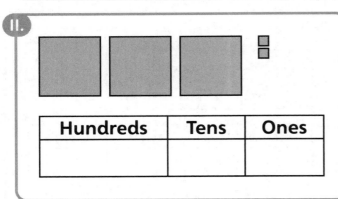

Hundreds	Tens	Ones

12.

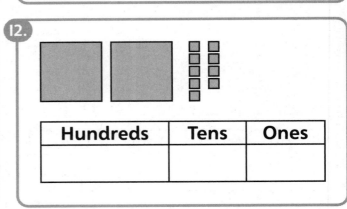

Hundreds	Tens	Ones

◯ Draw the number of blocks shown in the base ten chart.

13.

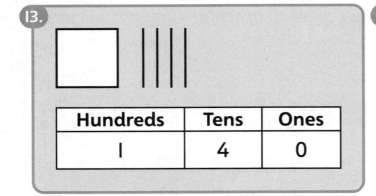

Hundreds	Tens	Ones
1	4	0

14.

Hundreds	Tens	Ones
3	2	0

15.

Hundreds	Tens	Ones
2	0	7

16.

Hundreds	Tens	Ones
1	0	4

Count the hundreds, tens, and ones blocks.

Write the number.

17.

	Hundreds	Tens	Ones	Number
	1	4	5	145

○ Fill in the table.

	Hundreds	Tens	Ones	Number
	1	3	7	137
	1	4	2	
				246
	2	0	8	
				330
	0	4	5	

59. Expanded Form

◯ Write what the digit 4 stands for.

1.	2.	3.	4.	5.	6.
245	431	994	734	947	463
40	_____	_____	_____	_____	_____

◯ What does the underlined digit stand for?

7.	8.	9.	10.	11.	12.
<u>6</u>53	<u>5</u>37	<u>9</u>78	7<u>3</u>4	4<u>5</u>2	58<u>9</u>
600	_____	_____	30	_____	_____

13.	14.	15.	16.	17.	18.
95<u>1</u>	32<u>6</u>	29<u>2</u>	9<u>6</u>8	<u>3</u>72	76<u>1</u>
_____	_____	_____	_____	_____	_____

19. BONUS	20. BONUS	21. BONUS
2<u>2</u>2 _____	2<u>2</u>2 _____	2<u>2</u>2 _____

◯ Fill in the blanks for the base ten names.

22.

749 = ___7___ hundreds + ___4___ tens + ___9___ ones

23.

835 = _____ hundreds + _____ tens + _____ ones

24.

301 = _____ hundreds + _____ tens + _____ one

25.

120 = _____ hundred + _____ tens + _____ ones

○ Fill in the blanks for the expanded form.

26.
749 = 700 + __40__ + 9

27.
873 = 800 + _____ + 3

28.
531 = _____ + 30 + 1

29.
492 = _____ + 90 + 2

30.
628 = 600 + 20 + _____

31.
341 = 300 + 40 + _____

32.
197 = ____ + ____ + ____

33.
246 = ____ + ____ + ____

34.
863 = ____ + ____ + ____

35.
752 = ____ + ____ + ____

○ Write the total.

36.
600 + 50 + 3 = __653__

37.
900 + 70 + 5 = _____

38.
500 + 90 + 7 = _____

39.
200 + 80 + 2 = _____

40.
300 + 20 + 4 = _____

41.
100 + 40 + 6 = _____

42.
800 + 10 + 9 = _____

43.
700 + 30 + 1 = _____

☐ Write the total.

44. 2 hundreds + 4 tens + 5 ones

_245_

45. 4 hundreds + 8 tens + 7 ones

_____

46. 6 hundreds + 3 tens + 1 one

_____

47. 8 hundreds + 1 ten + 8 ones

_____

☐ Write the total.

48.
```
  600
+  50
+   3
─────
  653
```

49.
```
  600
+  50
─────
```

50.
```
  600

+   3
─────
```

51.
```
  800
+  20
+   7
─────
```

52.
```
  800
+  20
─────
```

53.
```
  800

+   7
─────
```

54. 200 + 40 = _____

55. 300 + 60 = _____

56. 700 + 10 = _____

57. 200 + 4 = _____

58. 300 + 6 = _____

59. 700 + 1 = _____

60. 400 + 50 = _____

61. 500 + 7 = _____

62. 900 + 3 = _____

63. 100 + 80 = _____

64. 600 + 5 = _____

65. 400 + 70 = _____

66.

Ben says 600 + 5 = 650. Explain his mistake.

60. Adding 3-Digit Numbers

☐ Add by counting on.

1. 21 + 5 = _____

2. 91 + 7 = _____

3. 85 + 2 = _____

4. 121 + 5 = _____

5. 191 + 7 = _____

6. 285 + 2 = _____

7. 35 + 6 = _____

8. 74 + 8 = _____

9. 69 + 5 = _____

10. 135 + 6 = _____

11. 274 + 8 = _____

12. 769 + 5 = _____

☐ Write the number of hundreds, tens, and ones.

☐ Add.

13.

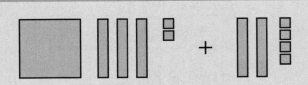

___*1*___ hundred and ___*5*___ tens and ___*6*___ ones = ___*156*___

14.

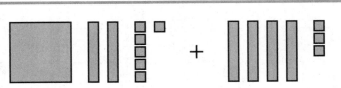

_____ hundred and _____ tens and _____ ones = _____

15.

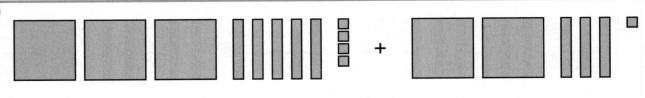

_____ hundreds and _____ tens and _____ ones = _____

◯ Write the numbers that the blocks show.
◯ Use the blocks to help you add.

16.

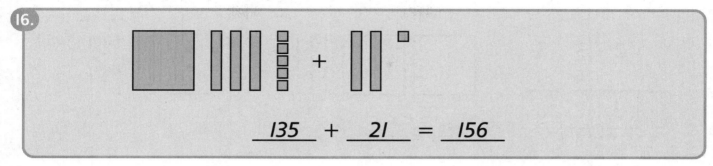

_135_ + _21_ = _156_

17.

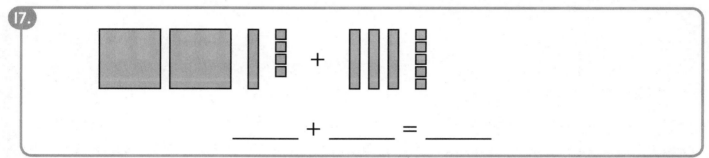

_____ + _____ = _____

18.

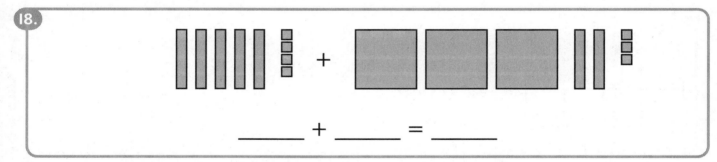

_____ + _____ = _____

19.

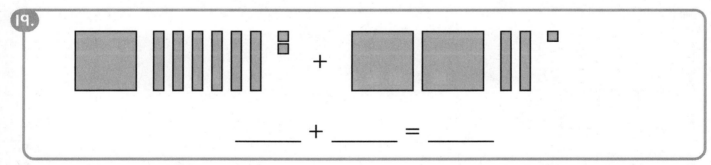

_____ + _____ = _____

20.

_____ + _____ = _____

○ Draw hundreds, tens, and ones to show the numbers.
○ Use the picture to help you add.

21.

```
  2 3 5
+ 1 4 3
-------
  3 7 8
```

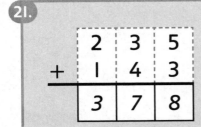

22.

```
  1 2 4
+ 2 3 1
-------
```

23.

```
  3 2 6
+ 1 2 3
-------
```

24.

```
  1 5 2
+ 1 2 4
-------
```

25. BONUS

The mother panda eats 243 pounds of bamboo a week. The father panda eats 254 pounds of bamboo a week. How much bamboo do they eat altogether?

JUMP Math Accumula

61. Using Place Value to Add (No Regrouping)

☐ Use the blocks to add.

1.

$$
\begin{array}{r}
3\ 4\ 5 \\
+\ 2\ 3\ 4 \\
\hline
5\ 7\ 9
\end{array}
$$

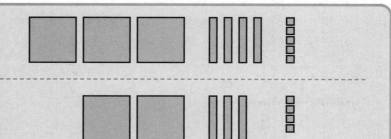

2.

$$
\begin{array}{r}
3\ 2\ 4 \\
+\ 3\ 5\ 1 \\
\hline

\end{array}
$$

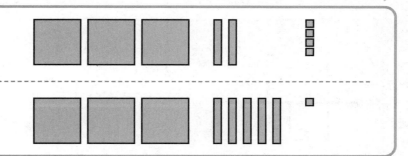

3.

$$
\begin{array}{r}
2\ 7\ 5 \\
+\ 4\ 1\ 4 \\
\hline

\end{array}
$$

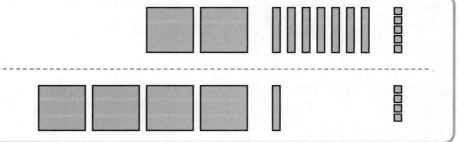

4.

$$
\begin{array}{r}
3\ 0\ 6 \\
+\ 4\ 7\ 1 \\
\hline

\end{array}
$$

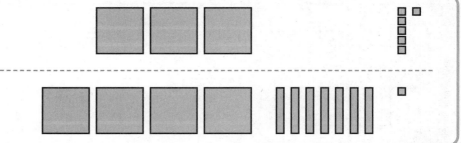

5.

$$
\begin{array}{r}
5\ 5\ 3 \\
+\ \ \ 2\ 5 \\
\hline

\end{array}
$$

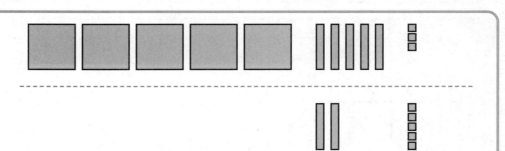

Draw hundreds, tens, and ones to show the addition.

Use the picture to add.

6.

	2	4	3
+	3	2	5
	5	6	8

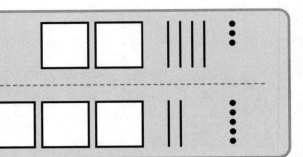

7.

	4	5	2
+	2	3	4

8.

	3	3	7
+	1	2	1

9.

	5	2	3
+	3	1	4

10.

	4	6	1
+	3	0	5

Add the ones. Add the tens. Add the hundreds.

11.

```
    2  5  3
+   4  2  6
─────────────
    6  7  9
```

12.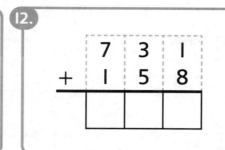

```
    7  3  1
+   1  5  8
─────────────
```

13.

```
    6  4  1
+   1  3  2
─────────────
```

14.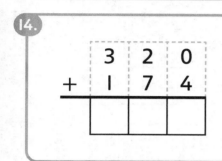

```
    3  2  0
+   1  7  4
─────────────
```

15.

```
    4  8  1
+   5  0  6
─────────────
```

16.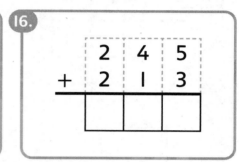

```
    2  4  5
+   2  1  3
─────────────
```

Use the grid to write the addition.
Add.

17.

325 + 304

```
    3  2  5
+   3  0  4
─────────────
    6  2  9
```

18.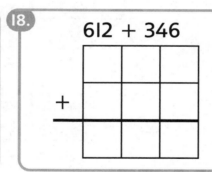

612 + 346

19.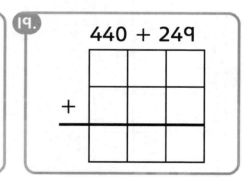

440 + 249

20.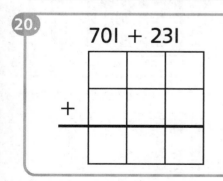

701 + 231

21.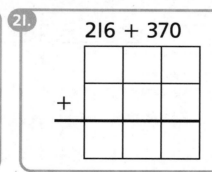

216 + 370

22.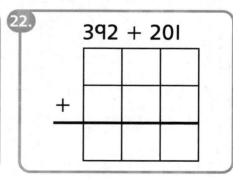

392 + 201

23.

There are 127 ants in one colony and 231 ants in another. How many ants are there altogether?

62. Using Base Ten Blocks to Add (Regrouping)

☐ Use the blocks to add.
☐ Write I to show regrouping.

1.

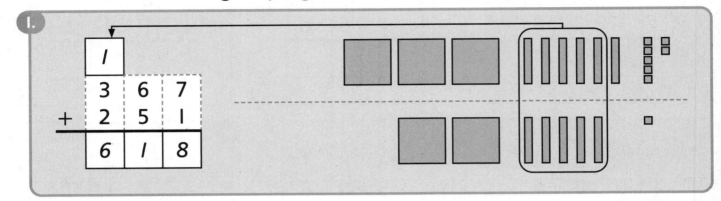

		1		
	3	6	7
+	2	5	1
	6	1	8

2.

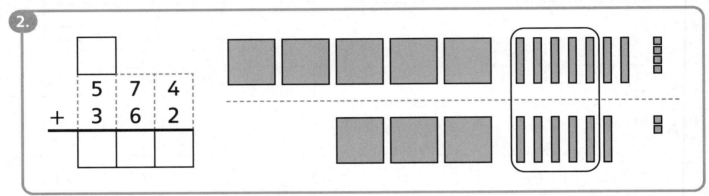

	5	7	4
+	3	6	2

3.

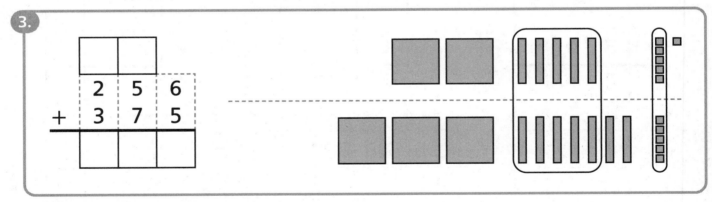

	2	5	6
+	3	7	5

4. BONUS

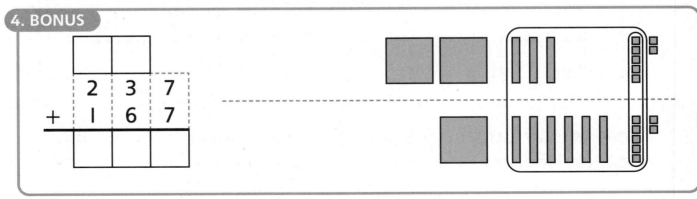

	2	3	7
+	1	6	7

☐ Regroup the tens.
☐ Add.

5.

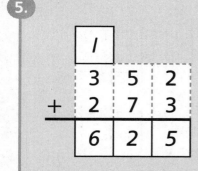

1		
3	5	2
+ 2	7	3
6	2	5

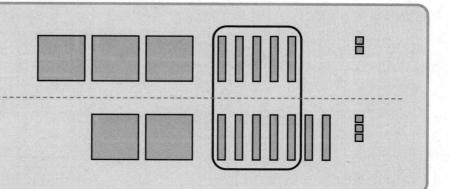

6.

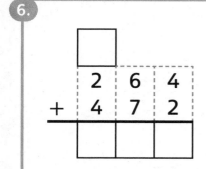

2	6	4
+ 4	7	2

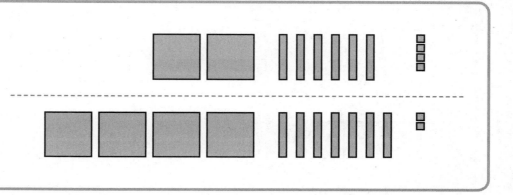

7.

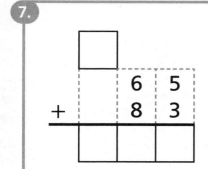

	6	5
+	8	3

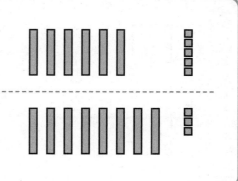

8. BONUS

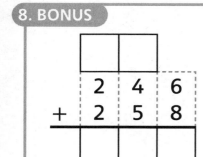

2	4	6
+ 2	5	8

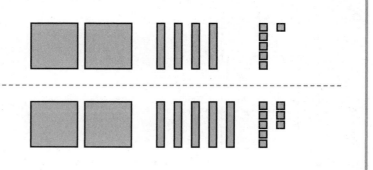

◯ Draw hundreds, tens, and ones. Show the regrouping.

◯ Add.

9.

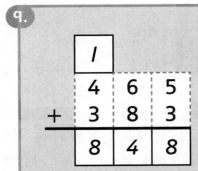

	1	
4	6	5
+ 3	8	3
8	4	8

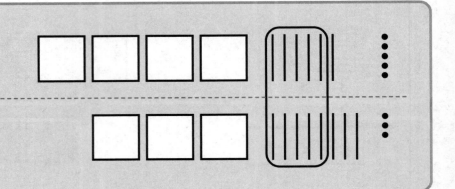

10.

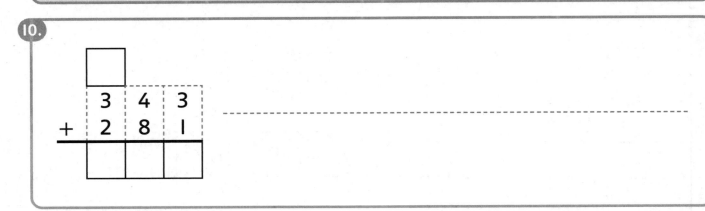

3	4	3
+ 2	8	1

11.

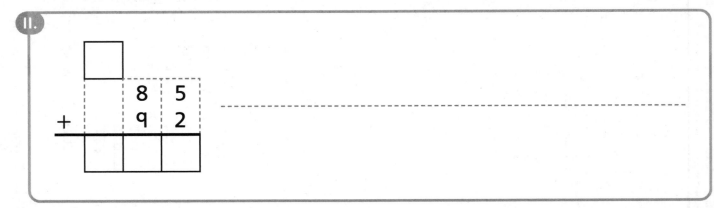

	8	5
+	9	2

12. BONUS

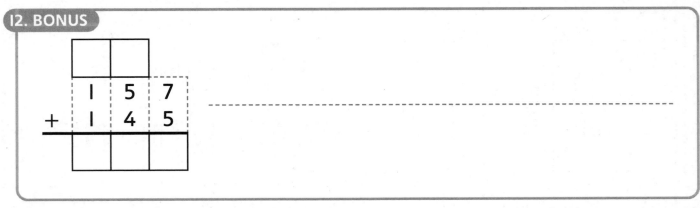

1	5	7
+ 1	4	5

63. Using Strategies to Add

◯ Write the missing number.

1. $498 + \underline{\ 2\ } = 500$

2. $397 + \underline{\hspace{1cm}} = 400$

3. $692 + \underline{\hspace{1cm}} = 700$

4. $791 + \underline{\hspace{1cm}} = 800$

5. $293 + \underline{\hspace{1cm}} = 300$

6. $194 + \underline{\hspace{1cm}} = 200$

7. $595 + \underline{\hspace{1cm}} = 600$

8. $899 + \underline{\hspace{1cm}} = 900$

9. $496 + \underline{\hspace{1cm}} = 500$

◯ Fill in the blanks so that the first two numbers add to a multiple of 100.

◯ Add to make the next multiple of 100.

10.
$498 \quad + \quad 7$
$= 498 + \underline{\ 2\ } + \underline{\ 5\ }$
$= 500 + \underline{\ 5\ }$

11.
$393 \quad + \quad 9$
$= 393 + \underline{\ 7\ } + \underline{\hspace{0.7cm}}$
$= 400 + \underline{\hspace{0.7cm}}$

12.
$697 \quad + \quad 5$
$= 697 + \underline{\ 3\ } + \underline{\hspace{0.7cm}}$
$= 700 + \underline{\hspace{0.7cm}}$

13.
$396 \quad + \quad 7$
$= 396 + \underline{\hspace{0.7cm}} + \underline{\hspace{0.7cm}}$
$= \underline{\hspace{1cm}} + \underline{\hspace{0.7cm}}$

14.
$798 \quad + \quad 6$
$= 798 + \underline{\hspace{0.7cm}} + \underline{\hspace{0.7cm}}$
$= \underline{\hspace{1cm}} + \underline{\hspace{0.7cm}}$

15.
$495 \quad + \quad 9$
$= 495 + \underline{\hspace{0.7cm}} + \underline{\hspace{0.7cm}}$
$= \underline{\hspace{1cm}} + \underline{\hspace{0.7cm}}$

16.
$597 \quad + \quad 4$
$= 597 + \underline{\hspace{0.7cm}} + \underline{\hspace{0.7cm}}$
$= \underline{\hspace{1cm}} + \underline{\hspace{0.7cm}}$

17.
$899 \quad + \quad 8$
$= 899 + \underline{\hspace{0.7cm}} + \underline{\hspace{0.7cm}}$
$= \underline{\hspace{1cm}} + \underline{\hspace{0.7cm}}$

18.
$294 \quad + \quad 8$
$= 294 + \underline{\hspace{0.7cm}} + \underline{\hspace{0.7cm}}$
$= \underline{\hspace{1cm}} + \underline{\hspace{0.7cm}}$

- ☐ Fill in the blanks so that the first two numbers add to a multiple of 100.
- ☐ Add to make the next multiple of 100.
- ☐ Add.

19.

$396 \quad + \quad 7$

$= 396 + \underline{\ 4\ } + \underline{\ 3\ }$

$= \underline{\ 400\ } + \underline{\ 3\ }$

$= \underline{\ 403\ }$

20.

$798 \quad + \quad 6$

$= 798 + \underline{\quad} + \underline{\quad}$

$= \underline{\ 800\ } + \underline{\quad}$

$= \underline{\quad}$

21.

$597 \quad + \quad 4$

$= 597 + \underline{\quad} + \underline{\quad}$

$= \underline{\quad} + \underline{\quad}$

$= \underline{\quad}$

22.

$899 \quad + \quad 8$

$= 899 + \underline{\quad} + \underline{\quad}$

$= \underline{\quad} + \underline{\quad}$

$= \underline{\quad}$

23.

$193 \quad + \quad 9$

$= 193 + \underline{\quad} + \underline{\quad}$

$= \underline{\quad} + \underline{\quad}$

$= \underline{\quad}$

24.

$697 \quad + \quad 4$

$= 697 + \underline{\quad} + \underline{\quad}$

$= \underline{\quad} + \underline{\quad}$

$= \underline{\quad}$

25. BONUS

$597 \quad + \quad 14$

$= 597 + \underline{\ 3\ } + \underline{\ 11\ }$

$= \underline{\quad} + \underline{\quad}$

$= \underline{\quad}$

26. BONUS

$899 \quad + \quad 58$

$= 899 + \underline{\quad} + \underline{\quad}$

$= \underline{\quad} + \underline{\quad}$

$= \underline{\quad}$

◯ Add.

27.

793 + 8 = __793__ + __7__ + __1__

= __800__ + __1__

= __801__

28.

897 + 6 = _____ + ___ + ___

= _____ + _____

= _____

29.

596 + 36 = _____ + ___ + ___

= _____ + _____

= _____

30.

498 + 57 = _____ + ___ + ___

= _____ + _____

= _____

31.

495 + 9

32.

294 + 8

33.

396 + 6

34.

694 + 7

35.

297 + 36

36.

398 + 25

37.

797 + 66

38.

893 + 99

39. BONUS

Anna wants to collect 500 stamps. She has 496 stamps in her book. Peter gives her 7 more stamps. How many more than 500 stamps does Anna have now?

40. BONUS

Paul says that 395 + 8 is the same as 400 + 3.
Is he correct? Explain.